HAUNTED
NORWICH

HAUNTED
NORWICH

DAVID CHISNELL

The
History
Press

Frontispiece: *Elm Hill, one of the most haunted streets in Norwich.*

First published in 2005 by Tempus Publishing
Reprinted 2006, 2007

Reprinted in 2012 by
The History Press
The Mill, Brimscombe Port,
Stroud, Gloucestershire, GL5 2QG
www.thehistorypress.co.uk

Reprinted 2013

© David Chisnell, 2012

The right of David Chisnell to be identified as the Author
of this work has been asserted in accordance with the
Copyrights, Designs and Patents Act 1988.

British Library Cataloguing in Publication Data.
A catalogue record for this book is available from the British Library.

ISBN 978 07524 3700 2

Typesetting and origination by
Tempus Publishing
Printed in Great Britain

CONTENTS

David Chisnell.

To my children Richard, Tom and Alice, who have helped me bring these stories to life on the City Ghost Walks over the last eight years.

INTRODUCTION

When I was first approached by Tempus Publishing to write a book on haunted Norwich, I was delighted to be asked. I've been running Ghost Walks around Norwich for the last eight years and telling people about the more macabre side of the city's history has become a passion of mine.

When I first began to research stories for my walks, I was surprised at the number of reported sightings, feelings and just general unusual goings-on that existed. It seemed you couldn't open a book at the library without finding a new 'ghost', and everybody wanted to tell their own supernatural story.

We had to pick and choose the stories we could tell on the walks, but the great thing about this book is that it has allowed me to pass on all the stories which I've uncovered over the last eight years.

As I've worked on the book, I've been amazed to be reminded of just how many stories there are to tell about our wonderful city. Surely Norwich must be one of the most haunted cities in the UK.

I am convinced that, after reading the stories in this book, you will agree that ghosts really do exist, and that a large number of them are 'alive and well' in Norwich.

Norwich Cathedral.

ONE

LORD SHEFFIELD
AND THE
ADAM AND EVE

Standing in the shadow of the cathedral, the Adam and Eve is the oldest known public house in Norwich. As long ago as 1249, workmen helping to rebuild parts of the cathedral after a major fire came to this very inn to be paid for their labours in beer and bread. But it was exactly 300 years later, in 1549, that the ghost of Lord Sheffield came to haunt the inn.

Shortly before he died, King Henry VIII made some very unpopular laws. Possibly the most unpopular one of all was the one that became known as the Enclosure Law, which allowed landowners to fence off common land and stop the local people from grazing their sheep and cattle. As you can imagine, this led to riots up and down the country. The biggest riot of all took place in Norwich and was led by a man by the name of Robert Kett.

Now, surprisingly enough, Kett was a landowner himself and had enclosed common land around his own estate. However, when he saw how the local townsfolk were suffering, he ripped down his fences and, accompanied by his brother William, led a march on Norwich demanding that the law be overturned and all enclosure fences taken down.

Kett came from a small town called Wymondham, which lies approximately 7 miles from Norwich. When he left Wymondham in July 1549, he had just seven people with him. Three weeks later, he was camped on the Mousehold Hills overlooking the city centre with an army in excess of 15,000, which gives some indication of how unpopular this particular law had become.

An army, led by Lord Sheffield, was sent from London to overthrow Kett and his rebels and for the next week or so Kett's rebels made various raids into the city, fighting the King's army wherever they could find them. Sure enough, on 1 August 1549, Robert Kett and his army came face to face with the army of the King, led by Lord Sheffield, along Bishopsgate, just 100 yards or so along from the Adam and Eve.

Imagine the scene: Robert Kett and his army coming in one direction, the King's army in the other. There was going to be a battle. A battle did indeed break out and, as it progressed, it soon became apparent that Lord Sheffield was going to lose. Sensing defeat, Sheffield did the only thing he could think of: he removed his helmet to reveal his identity, hoping, no doubt, to be taken hostage. However, things didn't quite work out that way and a butcher by the name of Ffoulks decided that he would rather have a famous scalp than a famous hostage and he slashed Sheffield across the side of his neck with his meat cleaver.

Lord Sheffield fell dying from his horse, the rest of the King's army fled and Kett and his army returned to Mousehold to celebrate, leaving Sheffield bleeding to death where he had fallen. The

King's army returned to find their leader barely alive. They carried him into the Adam and Eve and laid him across one of the tables, which is where he died. Ever since, it has been claimed that the Adam and Eve is haunted by the ghost of Lord Sheffield. He haunts the area where he was slain, he haunts the car park outside the pub and he haunts the entrance to the riverside walk. But most of all he haunts the pub itself.

If you ever get the chance to visit the Adam and Eve, the first thing you will notice is how small the bars are. Barely any structural changes have been made since its construction back in 1249. The main bar is particularly small and you would imagine that should somebody tap you on the shoulder you would see whoever had tapped you standing behind you when you turned round. Successive landlords have lost count of the number of times customers claim to have been tapped on the shoulder and yet when they've turned round the only thing behind them is a brick wall. We believe, of course, that it's Lord Sheffield who does the tapping.

Also, should you place something down on your table – car keys, cigarette lighter or mobile phone – and leave them unattended for a few moments, it's quite likely that when you return you will find they have vanished. You can turn the pub upside down and never find them and yet they will mysteriously reappear exactly where you left them a few days later. Either they have a very clever dog in the pub or, again, it is the work of Lord Sheffield.

Talk to any of the young girls who work in the pub and, almost without exception, they will tell you of the times they have been walking up the stairs from the cellar to the bar carrying a crate of beer or a box of crisps when an unseen hand has been run through their hair. When they tell you the tales, they won't bat an eyelid; the ghost is like an old friend of the family.

In the 1980s, an elderly blind gentleman was having his dinner in a side bar of the pub. There was nobody else in the bar except this gentleman and his guide dog. Suddenly, the barmaid heard a crash of crockery and saw the guide dog come racing out of the room. He was followed rapidly by the blind gentleman, who collided with the doorframe. When the gentleman had finally regained his composure, he told the barmaid how he had suddenly become aware of somebody joining him in the bar and had then felt a shiver as cold as ice as whatever it was had passed right through him. The entrance to the side bar was in full view of the barmaid from behind the counter and she swore that nobody else had entered the room.

In the downstairs bar, there are a number of silver tankards hanging above the counter. Occasionally, these tankards begin to swing from side to side as if pushed by an unseen hand. There is no wind and no reason for them to move and yet if they are stopped they will simply begin to swing again a few moments later. One evening when there were around a dozen young

A brick marks the spot where Lord Sheffield was killed during Kett's rebellion.

The Adam and Eve public house, which has been haunted by Lord Sheffield since 1549.

students in the bar, one of them noticed that while the tankards weren't swinging, something was dripping from one of them. He pointed it out to his friends and they all watched as it continued to drip, splashing on the counter below. After it had done this several times, one of the students went over to see what is was. Imagine his surprise when he found that not only was the tankard bone dry but so was the counter immediately below it.

That's the work of Lord Sheffield.

But what, I hear you ask, happened to Robert Kett? Well, Kett was destined to meet his own unfortunate end and to provide us with another possible ghost.

Having taken control of the city following the defeat of Lord Sheffield, Kett and his followers did little damage to it. For the most part, their protest was peaceful, their aim simply being to get the Enclosure Law repealed. However, it was decided to send another army to take on the forces of Robert Kett. This time, the army was led by the Earl of Warwick and the result was very different. The Earl of Warwick was a real man of war: he had his own private army amounting to around 8,000 soldiers. He was also accompanied by the army of Lord Manchester, who had recently fought and defeated the Scots just north of Newcastle. He also had around 5,000 German and Italian mercenaries with him. In all, an army approaching 17,000 soldiers made its way to take on the army of Robert Kett. They were practically all on horseback and had all the latest weapons of war: rifles and cannons, pikes, shields and staffs.

Robert Kett and his men had a few horses and one or two guns, stolen from Lord Sheffield and his men. They had meat cleavers and knives and they had pointed sticks. To say a battle took place just outside the city in an area known as Dussingdale would be wrong: it wasn't a battle, it was a massacre. The army of Robert Kett was slaughtered by the army of the King.

After several hours of fighting, around 3-4,000 bodies lay dead on the ground, the vast majority belonging to the army of Robert Kett. The rest of Kett's army fled. Robert Kett and his brother William were captured and taken to London and thrown in the Tower. The day after the battle, to teach the rebels a lesson, Warwick had 300 men hanged from the Magdalen Street gates of the city wall. They hanged 300 men in one day and they used one rope. Work it out for yourselves: even if it took ten hours to hang them all, it meant they were hanging somebody every two minutes.

Robert Kett and his brother were tried for treason and, of course, found guilty. The sentence passed on them was that they should be taken to 'a place of execution' which, in 1549, would have been Tyburn. There they were to be hanged by the neck and, while they were still alive, their innards were to be removed from their bodies. Their heads would then be cut from their shoulders and the bodies cut into four pieces. The heads would then be displayed on Tower Bridge while their quartered bodies would be displayed at the gates to the city to deter any other would-be rebels.

In 1549, the King of England was Edward VI, a young lad just eleven years old, and the country was being run by Lord Somerset. Somerset decided that it would be better for the Kett brothers to be executed in front of the people they had tried to overthrow and so, in December 1549, Robert and William Kett were brought back to Norwich and placed inside the Guildhall. A few days later, William Kett was returned to Wymondham, where he was hanged from the abbey steeple, and Robert Kett was taken to the city castle.

You may think it's not that far from the Guildhall to the castle, possibly no more than a couple of hundred yards. However, you might think it was a little further if, like Robert Kett, you were dragged there by a horse with your arms and legs in chains and wearing only your everyday

The Magdalen Street gates, where 300 rebels were hanged in one day.

Robert Kett met his undignified death on this castle wall.

clothes. Once he reached the castle, Kett was placed against the wall facing the marketplace. A rope was lowered from the battlements and a noose at the end of it was placed around his neck – not tightly enough to kill him. His body was then hauled up by the neck to the battlements at the top of the castle, where his body was fixed to a gibbet, a wooden or metal pole sticking out between two of the battlements. Still in chains, he was left to hang alive. Because it was winter when he was hanged, his body was painted with pitch and tar before being hauled to the top of the castle so that he would survive a little longer.

The worst part of being hanged in chains may well have been that it left you unable to protect yourself from the birds that swooped around the battlements. It is almost certain that Kett would have lost his eyes to the birds long before he died.

There is no definite record of how long Kett remained on the wall. We know he was hanged at the start of December 1549 and there is an entry in the mayor's yearbook the following April which claims: 'Kett's body remains on the wall for winter store'. It is obvious he was there for some time. His body would have simply slowly fallen apart and landed on to the ground below. We don't believe he was ever buried and can only assume that his remains were burnt in the ditches, along with any Lollards or witches who happened to be passing through.

Four hundred years later, in 1949, a plaque was erected on to the castle wall proclaiming: 'Our Great Hero, Robert Kett'. It's strange how 400 years of history can alter someone's standing. It is said Kett can still be found wandering around the loading bays of the Castle Mall Shopping Centre, built immediately under the castle where he was hanged. Almost as soon as work began on the project, there were reports of an odd character in medieval clothing wandering around the building site. At the time, it was generally thought to be a local homeless person looking for somewhere to rest his head. However, the reports continued once the complex was complete. Regular sightings of the character were reported, always in the bays at the rear of the complex, just below the very wall where Kett was hanged.

TWO

THE STORY OF
WILLIAM SHEWARD

Just around the corner from the Adam and Eve, along what is now part of Bishopsgate, is a wall standing in front of the local magistrates' court. In the mid-1800s, there was a small row of terraced houses where the wall now stands. It was known as Tabernacle Street and there was, in fact, a tabernacle standing at the end of the row, opposite the Adam and Eve.

On Sunday 15 June 1851, while local members of the tabernacle congregation were joined in prayer, something far more sinister was happening in one of the houses just along the street. The full details of what was taking place in the upstairs bedroom that afternoon would not emerge for another eighteen years and those who passed by on their way to the riverside could not have guessed at the terrible tragedy that was unfolding.

The house was owned by William Sheward, who lived alone with his wife Martha. William Sheward was thirty-five years old while Martha was fifty-four, and it would appear that the attraction of being married to an older woman had worn a little bit thin. Following an argument over money, William Sheward went to the bathroom, where he kept his trusty cut-throat razor. Creeping up behind his wife, he quickly slit her throat from ear to ear, allowing her dead body to fall to the bedroom floor.

As if this wasn't bad enough, our story now takes a twist that defies imagination. Faced with the problem of a dead body to dispose of, Sheward came up with an idea of how to make his task a little easier. Perhaps it should be pointed out here what Sheward's profession was. He wasn't a doctor, he certainly wasn't a surgeon, he wasn't even a butcher and, as far as we know, he had no dissection skills whatsoever. He was, in fact, a pawnbroker, working at a local shop close to the city castle. However, this evident lack of medical knowledge didn't deter him. Believing that it would be easier to dispose of the body in smaller sections, he set about the task of cutting it into small pieces using the very same cut-throat razor. It took him four nights to complete his task, first taking off the head, then the arms and legs and finally cutting up the torso itself.

It was at this point, surrounded by small pieces of his wife's body, that Sheward hit upon another idea. Wouldn't it be easier to get rid of the body if it was softer? Fetching his largest saucepan from the kitchen, Sheward set about the second stage of his operation: boiling the body parts over the open fire to soften them up. This part of the plan took a further three nights, by which time, by his own admission, he was having to throw lavender leaves on the fire to get rid of the smell. An 'amusing' aside came when his wife's sister came looking for Martha a few weeks later and found Sheward cooking his dinner in the very same saucepan. Let's hope he had washed it out in between!

Having now reduced his wife's body to small, soft pieces, Sheward set out on part three of his plan, with a nightly ritual so macabre it defies belief. For the next week, Sheward wandered round the streets of Norwich with a bucket. The bucket was covered with a tea towel and underneath the tea towel were bits and pieces of Martha. As he wandered the streets, he threw bits of the body out wherever he happened to be, an arm here, a foot there.

Not too surprisingly, parts began to turn up. First of all it was a hand, then a foot, then pieces of an arm and a leg. In fact, so many pieces were turning up that the police originally thought it was a practical joke being played by local medical students. However, they soon came to the grisly realisation that they were dealing with a particularly gruesome murder.

Never before had a crime attracted so much local attention. The local papers were full of the latest finds and stories of a 'monster' roaming the city streets spread like wildfire. People were urged to lock their doors as soon as it became dark until the offender was caught.

The only piece of the body that never turned up was the head and so there was no way of identifying it. Martha Sheward was not reported missing and, for some reason, the police surgeon had estimated the age of the female body to be no more than late teens or early twenties. There was nothing to connect William Sheward with the horrendous crime and it seemed as if he would get away with his foul deed. Eighteen years later, however, the truth was about to be revealed.

By 1868, William Sheward was living with his second wife above the Merchant Arms public house in St Martin at Oak, Norwich. However, New Year's Eve found him wandering the streets of south London, racked with guilt and convinced he was being pursued by the ghost of his dead wife. Finally, on Friday 1 January 1869, he walked into a police station in Walworth, where Inspector James Davies had come on duty an hour earlier.

Davies later said that in the eighteen years he had been in the police force he had never been involved with such a macabre case. He recalled that Sheward had approached the desk and stated that he wished to make a charge against himself. 'What is it?' Davies had asked. 'For the wilful murder of my first wife in Norwich,' replied Sheward. Over the next hour or so, he made a full confession but refused to go into great detail about what he had done, as it was 'too terrible'. A few days later, Sheward was brought back to Norwich, where he was taken straight to the local gaol and charged with murder.

By the time of his trial in March 1869, Sheward had withdrawn his confession, claiming that he had been depressed and drunk when he made it. He claimed that his wife had emigrated to Australia with another man many years earlier and that he had not seen or heard from her since.

The evidence against Sheward was very poor. Apart from his admission, there was nothing to tie him to the body parts found around the city. Furthermore, his wife had been fifty-four years old while the police surgeon had suggested that the victim was much, much younger. It was suggested by his defence that his original confession could have been provided by anyone who had read of the case in the local papers.

The judge also reminded the jury that no 'new' information had been offered by Sheward and he pointed out that if the defendant was entitled to be believed when he made the confession then he was just as entitled to be believed now when he withdrew it. However, he also told them that they had to ask themselves why anyone should have made up such a story if it was untrue. They should also consider the fact that all known evidence fitted comfortably with the confession and that although Sheward had pleaded not guilty he had refused to give any evidence during the trial.

The jury retired at 3.05 p.m. and returned with a verdict an hour and a quarter later. Perhaps it was the original confession that had swayed them, or the fact that Sheward had refused to

Tabernacle Street, the scene of Norwich's bloodiest murder.

give any evidence. Whatever it was, when the clerk asked them for their verdict the foreman replied, 'The jury find him guilty'. Sheward was then asked if he had anything to say as to why judgement according to the law should not be made. The prisoner replied, 'I have nothing to say.' Putting on the black cap, the judge then passed sentence, that Sheward should be 'taken to a place of execution and there be hanged by the neck until your body be dead'.

When Sheward arrived back at the city gaol to await execution, acute rheumatism in his ankles meant he was allowed to stay in the prison infirmary and was supported by warders wherever he went. Any lingering doubts over the guilty verdict were quashed once and for all when Sheward asked to see the prison governor on the afternoon of 15 April.

At the meeting, Sheward made a complete confession, describing in great detail all that he had done. He explained that he had argued with his wife over money that he had lent to his employer. When she had threatened to confront his employer and reclaim it, he was forced to stop her. He described how he had slit her throat, dismembered and boiled her body parts and then strewn those parts around the city under the cover of darkness. He gave permission for his confession to be passed to the Home Secretary and the trial judge but asked that it should not be made public until after his execution.

As Sheward awaited the date of his execution, the rheumatism in his ankles grew worse, causing him to be carried around the infirmary for most of the time. On the evening before the set date of execution, he wrote a last letter to his second wife in which he apologised and asked for forgiveness.

The following morning, Sheward rose at 5.30 a.m. and at 6.00 a.m. he was joined by the chaplain for prayer. Shortly before 7.45 a.m., Sheward and the chaplain were joined by chief prison warder Hall and another warder named Base. As the bells of St Peter Mancroft and St Giles joined those of the prison to toll the death strokes, Sheward, the two warders and the chaplain made their way to the iron gate between the governor's house and the gaol. Here they were met by the undersheriff and a local surgeon.

At this point, Sheward became unable to walk and had to be carried to the pinioning room by the warders. After the final adjustments had been made to the pinioning, Sheward gave a shudder which caused a tremor to pass through his entire body. According to one of the warders, the tremor stayed with Sheward until after he was hanged.

Supported by the warders, Sheward was led to the scaffold while the chaplain read the funeral service. Once upon the scaffold, Calcraft, the hangman, quickly fixed the cap and rope while Sheward prayed earnestly. Calcraft then withdrew the bolt and Sheward fell. A brief struggle brought life to an end.

As Sheward fell, the clocks were striking 8.00 a.m. and a black flag was hoisted to the top of the prison façade. William Sheward was only the second person to be hanged at the gaol and he would be the last. Furthermore, he was the first person to be executed in Norwich in private. A recent Home Office Bill had banned public executions because of the unruly and riotous behaviour which now generally attended these events.

However, the lure of a man being judicially killed was still enough to attract the general public. At 7.30 a.m. that morning, there had been just twenty or so people outside the prison gates. By the time the clocks struck 8.00 a.m., a crowd in excess of 2,000 were crowded around the entrance. Exactly one hour later, at 9.00 a.m., and long after the last ghoulish onlooker had left the area, Sheward's body was cut down. After being buried within the grounds of the gaol, a brick was marked with the initials W.S. and placed within the prison wall.

At last, some eighteen years after the event, the mystery of the unknown body, together with Sheward himself, could be laid to rest. The only remaining mystery was what had happened to Martha Sheward's head. Sheward had admitted severing it from the body and boiling it in the saucepan but refused to tell what had happened to it after that. Who knows – all that cutting and boiling must have been hard work and, no doubt, Sheward must have built up quite an appetite by the end of it.

Walkers along the riverside just around the corner from the old tabernacle often tell of a mysterious figure seen lurking in the hedgerow. Some describe him as a haunted-looking figure and others claim to have seen him carrying what appears to be a bucket. Could the ghost of William Sheward still be repenting his actions of that Sunday afternoon in 1851?

THREE

TOMBLAND

Dark, shadowy, medieval and full of ghosts – without doubt, Tombland is the most haunted area of Norwich. Even its name, Tombland, makes the hairs stand up on the back of your neck. Tombland: 'a land full of tombs, a land full of bodies'. And while Tombland may indeed be full of bodies – dead, living and those in-between – its name means nothing more sinister than 'open space', the open space where the original city marketplace stood before the Normans moved it to its current position towards the end of the eleventh century.

It wasn't long before this 'open space' became an area of intense building work, with many famous city landmarks soon making their first appearance. Over the years, each building would gain its own tragic story of death and horror, and Tombland would acquire its reputation as the most haunted area of the city. An area so full of ghosts it seems almost impossible to walk from one side of it to the other without bumping into one of them.

Tombland has stood in the shadow of the cathedral for almost 900 years and has become home to many a ghost and horror story along the way. From the battles of Kett's rebellion to the skirmishes of the English Civil War, from the horrors of the plague to the persecution of religious nonconformists, it has found itself constantly surrounded by death and its aftermath.

The burning woman

One of the more unusual ghosts reported in Tombland is that of a young woman who has been seen almost 'floating' across the grounds of the cathedral. She has been described as being 'in a cloud' with her feet obscured by the mists that follow her. Could these 'mists', in fact, be smoke?

In the 1200s there was little love lost between the cathedral workers and the young men of the city. Fights and skirmishes often took place as the cathedral workers flouted their higher social standing and treated the more ordinary folk of the city as servants and slaves.

St George's church, which had been built as an alternative venue for worship opposite the cathedral, was often desecrated by the priory men. Feelings ran high and each side were constantly on the lookout for ways to upset the other.

By August 1272, matters were coming to a head and, following a series of fights and quarrels between the priory men and the local young men, a major battle threatened to take place at the annual Tombland Fair that month. On 7 August, priory men left the cathedral and robbed a local merchant. They then entered a local tavern and drank the wine without offering payment, before returning to their cloisters in a drunken stupor.

Before they left the inn, they turned over barrels of beer and laughed and jeered at the innkeeper as he watched, powerless to stop them.

When the Bishop discovered what had happened, he feared revenge attacks and ordered that the cathedral gates should be closed and locked the following day. His fears were well founded: the next day, learning of the previous evening's incidents, a group of young men tried to force their way into the cathedral grounds. Failing to break down the gates, they came up with another plan. Climbing to the top of St George's church, they began to shoot slings of fire into the cathedral grounds. Some of these fireballs landed on the thatched roofs of the buildings inside the cathedral grounds and fires quickly broke out. As the monks and their servants tried to put out the flames, a woman set fire to the main cathedral gates. As the fire weakened the bolts, a mob of locals charged the gates with tables from the local taverns and eventually the gates were ripped from their hinges. The crowd now entered the cathedral grounds, determined to wreak as much damage as possible. Over the next few hours, hoards of gold and silver were plundered from the cathedral and many of the monks' and servants' quarters were set ablaze. A number of monks were killed with lances, while many more hid or fled in fear.

When calm had finally been restored, the incident was reported to Rome by the Bishop and the Pope issued a papal bull commanding the authorities to punish those involved. In 1272, the civic authorities would have had no choice but to obey the bull and a dreadful revenge was exacted. Thirty-four offenders were tied to horses and dragged around the streets of the city between Tombland and the marketplace until they were dead. Many others were publicly whipped in the market place; the whipping was conducted by the priory men, who no doubt carried out the punishment with great enthusiasm.

Cathedral Close, where a woman walks with her feet covered by mist.

The young woman who had set fire to the cathedral gates was identified and brought before the Bishop. A few days later, she was tied to a stake inside the cathedral grounds and burnt alive before a horrified crowd. Could this young woman be the same one who, even now, is seen in the grounds with her feet covered by 'mist'?

The case of Walter Eghe

The story of Walter Eghe is not a ghost story in the strictest sense, but is definitely a case of somebody coming back from the dead.

Built in the thirteenth century, St George's church in Tombland provided an alternative place for worship to the imposing cathedral opposite. However, it also served a more macabre purpose. St George's graveyard was the official burial place for convicted and hanged criminals and, following their execution, the criminals' bodies would be brought to St George's to be laid in their final resting place.

St George's church, where Walter Eghe came back from the dead.

In 1286, a local man by the name of Walter Eghe had been found in possession of stolen goods. He claimed he had bought them in good faith from another man in a local pub, but he was taken to the castle and charged. Although the evidence against him was flimsy, the fact that he was found in possession was enough for the local magistrates to find him guilty. The law, at that time, allowed for one punishment only for theft, that of hanging, and Walter Eghe was sentenced to die at the end of a rope.

Despite his furious protestations and appeals from many of his friends and family, the sentence was carried out and Eghe was hanged on the banks of the castle mound. After a short while, his body was cut down, thrown into a cart and taken the short distance to St George's church. A grave had already been dug and all that remained was for his body to be placed inside the coffin and buried. The burial men laid his body on a slab inside the church while they went to fetch the coffin. However, when they returned they were in for quite a shock. Having fully regained consciousness, Walter Eghe was now sitting up on the slab demanding to be told where he was. When it was explained to him what had happened, he declared that he had been spared by the grace of God himself.

The law did not allow for Eghe to be hanged again and it was decided that he should remain inside St George's until a decision on his future had been made. A few days later, Eghe managed to slip away unnoticed. He ran across Tombland, straight through the gates of the cathedral and into the cathedral itself, where he claimed sanctuary.

In 1272, if you were granted sanctuary by the Catholic Church it meant no one could remove you from their care and, following their recent disputes with the Church and people of the city, the monks saw this as a great way to make them both look rather foolish. Sanctuary was duly granted and Eghe remained inside the cathedral, despite the protests of the local judiciary.

Some months later, King Edward visited the city and he was made aware of the Walter Eghe case. After studying the evidence, the King decided that Walter Eghe had not been given a fair trial and that the evidence against him was far from conclusive. A full pardon was granted and Eghe left the cathedral to see out the rest of his life in peace. No doubt he always remembered just how close he had come to being buried alive in the grounds of St George's church. He remains the only person in history to have been hanged at the castle and lived to tell the tale.

The Maid's Head Hotel

From its earliest days, the Maid's Head has often found itself involved with various stories of ghosts and horror. It houses, of course, its very own ghost, believed to be that of a chambermaid previously employed at the hotel. Staff and guests will often claim to see the ghostly apparition of an elderly lady wandering around the hotel. Dressed all in grey, she appears to come up from the downstairs bar, through the swing doors and into the main hotel area. Always accompanied by the smell of lavender, she then wanders around the hotel, peeking into bedrooms as she goes. After a good look round, she returns to the downstairs bar, goes back through the swing doors, down the stairs and disappears back into the cellars. Her visits tend to coincide with any structural work or redecoration of the hotel, leading the staff to believe that she is simply checking that standards are being maintained for old times' sake.

Dating back to the thirteenth century, the Maid's Head was originally called the Myrtle Fish but this all changed following the visit of Queen Elizabeth I to the city in 1578. It is often claimed that the Queen stayed at the Maid's Head Hotel while she was in Norwich but it is far more likely that she stayed at the Bishop's Palace just a few yards around the corner. It is

The Maid's Head Hotel is haunted by an elderly chambermaid.

true, however, that the Queen attended a banquet held in her honour at the hotel while she was in Norwich.

Following the banquet, the Queen spoke very kindly of the hotel, claiming she had enjoyed the hospitality and the meal greatly. The owner of the Myrtle Fish, as it was still known, was a Dutch refugee by the name of Christopher Baret, who had arrived in Norwich some years earlier with Dutch refugees known as Strangers. The Strangers had brought their weaving skills from Holland with them and turned Norwich into a centre for the weaving and textile industry. So overwhelmed by the Queen's compliments was Baret, he announced that he would rename the hotel in the Queen's honour. Quite why he chose 'Maid's Head' as opposed to 'Queen's Head' is unknown but the new name was adopted within weeks of Elizabeth's exit from the city.

However, a far greater legacy of the Queen's visit was to overwhelm Norwich in the months to come. As Elizabeth and her entourage moved on across the country, a far less welcome reminder of her visit was already beginning to prowl the alleyways: the plague.

When Queen Elizabeth I came to Norwich in 1578, she brought all sorts of wonderful things with her. She brought fine food, she brought fine wine, she brought fancy clothes and she brought the plague. It is a fact that in almost every town or city the Queen visited that year, the plague broke out within weeks of her leaving. That is not to say that the Queen herself was a carrier, but it seems fairly certain that somebody who was travelling around the country with her was indeed carrying the plague with them.

During the plague in 1349, looters were dropped to their deaths from the battlements of St George's church.

Norwich suffered particularly badly from the effects of the plague of 1578. Between August that year and the following February, over 4,700 deaths were recorded in the city from the plague. If we add on all the ones that went unrecorded – people just passing through, people who had no fixed abode and those who were buried without being counted – it is estimated that as many as 7,000 or even 8,000 people may have died from the effects of the plague. Bearing in mind that the entire population of Norwich in 1578 was no more than 15-16,000, that meant nearly half the population of the city was lost in just six months.

This plague wasn't the first to visit Norwich. As long ago as 1349, the Black Death had been an unwelcome guest. When stories of the Black Death running amok in places such as Bristol in 1348 first reached the population of Norwich, they probably felt reasonably safe tucked away on the east coast. By the start of 1349, however, reports began circulating that the plague had reached London and fears started that it might indeed find its way to East Anglia.

Those fears were well founded and in March 1349 the dreaded Black Death swept into the city. Showing absolutely no mercy to young or old, fit or unwell, the plague threatened to wipe out the entire population as it raced through the alleyways. Those who did not die in the first few weeks were left with the task of burying their loved ones. As the number of victims grew, few formal burials took place. Bodies were piled on top of each other as the rats ran through the alleyways and the grim cry of 'Bring out your dead' rang through the city.

Cartload after cartload of bodies were taken to Cathedral Close in Tombland, as it was turned into a gigantic burial area. The name Tombland must have seemed even more sickeningly appropriate as the area became overrun with the hundreds of bodies arriving on a daily basis.

Cathedral Close, which became a giant plague pit during the 1300s.

Great pits were dug to bury them in; often those digging the pits would fall ill on their shovels and join the other victims a few hours later. Over two-thirds of the clergy died during the plague; many of them were buried in the graveyards next to and behind St George's. Many people have wondered why the graveyards are raised so high; it was simply to accommodate all the bodies.

But St George's was to have another, more terrifying, role to play during the plague. Those who weren't struck down by the disease often resorted to stealing from the bodies of the victims to help subsidise their own welfare. A ring here, a necklace there and, if you struck lucky, maybe a few coins to buy some food with. If the thief was caught, the penalty was severe. The looters would be taken to St George's church and pushed up a spiral staircase to the roof. Once on the roof, they would have their hands tied behind their backs and then their legs would be strapped together. They would then be turned upside down and dropped head first to the ground below, landing just to the side of the graveyard. Their bodies would then be recovered and, regardless of whether they were dead or still alive, they would be thrown into the pits with the rest of the plague victims and left.

By the time the Black Death had left the city, the population had fallen from 6,000 to just 2,000. The record books for the following year show only one-third of the market stalls being open for business. A similar account records the fact that many hundreds of houses stood empty in 1350.

It is hardly surprising, then, that panic swept through the city like wildfire when the first traces of the plague were again encountered in August 1578. Old pits were hastily reopened to house all the new dead bodies that the plague was expected to leave in its wake. This time, a new tactic was to be used to help slow down the spread of the disease. Instead of leaving bodies out on the streets to be collected by the pitmen, it was decided that when a family died their house would be sealed off. All the windows would be covered over, the doors barred from the outside and great red crosses of warning painted on the walls. The bailiffs would then return some time later with the pitmen to retrieve the bodies and bury them in the pits. A good idea, on the face of it, but it could go wrong and, when it did, it would leave catastrophic results, as our next ghost found out to her horror.

The Lady in Grey

Augustine Steward House stands in the middle of Tombland. Built in 1549 by Augustine Steward, it is the very house that Lord Sheffield stayed in the night before his ill-fated battle with Robert Kett. It is surrounded by the many pits dug to bury plague victims and, along with almost every other building in the area, was overwhelmed by the plague of 1578.

When it was believed that everybody in the house had succumbed to the plague, the bailiffs came and sealed the house up. Following the standard procedure, they locked and bolted the doors from the outside, boarded up the windows and painted red crosses over the paintwork to warn others to stay away.

Five, or maybe six, weeks later the bailiffs returned with the ever-present pitmen to remove the bodies from the house. It was then that the full horror of what had happened within the house was revealed.

As they were dragging out the bodies of the mother and father, the pitmen noticed some unusual marks on their legs. Upon closer inspection, these were discovered to be teeth marks and pieces of flesh appeared to have been bitten away from the limbs. The sense of horror increased when they realised that these teeth marks had not been made by the rats that often raced through the houses feeding on the dead bodies locked inside, but were in fact human teeth marks.

As the pitmen cautiously removed the rest of the bodies from the house, the full extent of what had happened became clear. Inside the mouth and throat of one of the daughters were pieces of dead human flesh. It seemed that the bailiffs had been a little premature in sealing up the house, as the young girl had still been alive. The horror she must have suffered can only be imagined. To have been locked in a house with no food or water and surrounded by the dead bodies of her family must have been awful enough. But to then have to feast on their plague-ridden bodies in an attempt to stay alive is beyond comprehension. Can there be a worse way to die than to choke on the flesh of your own dead parents?

Since that day, the ghost of the young girl has been reputed to haunt Augustine Steward House, the adjoining buildings and Tombland Alley, the alleyway that runs between the house and St George's church. She always appears dressed in faded, ragged clothes of grey and has, for that reason, become known as the Lady in Grey. Many occupants of the house, which has enjoyed a number of uses over the years, claim to have either seen or felt her presence. Moving objects around at night seems to be her favourite pastime. She has also been known to open and close doors, causing a breeze at the most inconvenient of times.

Others claim to have seen her walking up and down Tombland Alley, and even a vicar of St George's vouches for her existence. Reverend John Minns confirms that, as he practised his sermon for the weekend one day at the altar, he glanced up to see a young woman dressed in grey enter the church through the main doors. She then proceeded to walk across the back of the church and exit through the doors leading to Tombland Alley. She didn't bother to open the doors on the way, which was perhaps not too surprising, considering they had been sealed for many years.

When Samson and Hercules House, next door to Augustine Steward House, was a local dance hall known as Ritzy's, a disc jockey went upstairs one evening to investigate some strange noises. There was a private party being held at the dance hall that night and it was not unknown for youngsters to try and gain access via the toilet windows and then join the party, pretending to be a friend of a guest.

When the disc jockey made his way upstairs, he saw a young woman leaving the ladies' toilets. Dressed all in grey, she didn't look like the usual visitors to the club so he went to challenge her. Ignoring him completely, the young woman walked straight past him without a word. As he turned to see where she was going, he was amazed to see that she appeared to have no feet and was simply floating down the corridor. In something of a panic, he reported what he had seen to the manager, who told him, in no uncertain terms, that if he wished to keep his job he would not repeat the story to anybody else. The manager obviously felt that a ghost would be bad for business.

Samson and Hercules House

One of the largest plague pits in the city was dug beneath where Samson and Hercules House now stands. The Samson, as the house is affectionately known, has been a dance hall since the early 1900s. Many people dancing there will know that there is a swimming pool located immediately below the dance hall, but how many know they are dancing above an old plague pit containing what is left of somewhere in the region of 5,000 dead bodies? Does the phrase 'dancing on somebody's grave' suddenly spring to mind?

Augustine Steward House, home to the Lady in Grey.

Above: *Samson and Hercules House, where it's possible to dance on somebody's grave.*

Left: *The Take 5 café gets the occasional 'visitor' from Samson and Hercules House next door.*

We've already covered the Lady in Grey's visit to the Samson but other ghosts are also reputed to haunt the building. Because of the close proximity of the pit to the cathedral, many monks who died in the various plagues that came to the city are believed to be buried underneath the dance floor. Monks are a regular feature of life at Samson and Hercules House, and not just on fancy dress night either. Some years ago, a young female professor from Belgium came to deliver a lecture in one of the rooms at the top of the house. At the end of it, she asked the organisers why there had been four monks sitting so attentively in the back row. Surprisingly, nobody else had noticed them.

Before it became a dance hall, Samson and Hercules House was the home of the local YWCA. Many of the young girls who stayed there would claim to have a nightmare if they slept in the back bedroom on the top floor. The nightmare was always the same: being buried alive in a great pit of dead bodies. Now that we know what's underneath the house, perhaps we shouldn't be too surprised. By the time the house was sold to become a dance hall, that back bedroom had been sealed off and was no longer being used. Just how many people must have had the same nightmare before the YWCA would care to sacrifice a bedroom?

To the left of the Samson stands another building with its own tale to tell. The Take 5 café used to be the Louis Marchesi public house and it has its own ghost downstairs. The crypt below the public house dates back to the 1500s and is at the same level as the plague pit next door. Staff claim to regularly see the shadowy figure of a man appearing through the wall which separates the crypt and the old pit. Not one of our more interesting ghosts, he tends to come through the wall, stand and stare for a few moments and then fade back through the wall again. No doubt he is missing the company of his 5,000 bedfellows!

Sir Thomas Erpingham

The main entrance into Cathedral Close is through Erpingham Gate, named after Sir Thomas Erpingham of Norwich. Erpingham was born just around the corner from Tombland, in an area known as St Martin's at Palace Plain. As every Norfolk schoolchild will know, Sir Thomas led the archers at the Battle of Agincourt in 1415, a battle that culminated in one of the greatest victories by the English over their French enemies in history.

A close comrade of Sir Thomas was killed during the battle and his body was brought back to Norwich. It was entombed in the Carnary Chapel in Cathedral Close, just by the side of the cathedral. The Carnary Chapel itself has an unusual history. In the 1300s, it was discovered that Norwich was running out of suitable places to bury its dead. An ingenious plan was thought up: all the old bodies would be dug up to make room for the new ones. However, it was believed if you broke somebody's bones, you also broke their soul. Therefore all the bones had to be carefully packed away and stored. The Carnary Chapel was chosen as their final resting place and contains literally thousands of boxes containing countless bones from the past.

Back to Sir Thomas and his friend. Every year on 25 October, the anniversary of the battle, Sir Thomas would visit his friend's tomb and drink a toast to his health. As time went by, of course, Sir Thomas himself died. However, a little thing like that didn't stop him. Year after year, people would claim to see the ghost of Sir Thomas enter the Close through his own gateway and then continue into the Carnary Chapel. There he would continue to drink to his friend's good health.

Some years later, the tombs in the Carnary Chapel were moved to inside the cathedral itself. Sir Thomas was never to be seen again; it is a little worrying, perhaps, that the man who was chosen to lead the archers at Agincourt wasn't quite bright enough to find his way from one building to the one next door.

However, Sir Thomas wasn't the only ghost seen loitering around the gates.

Reverend Thomas Tunstall

During the reign of James I, a general persecution of Catholic believers took place. While those who practised their faith in private were usually allowed to go free, anyone found openly preaching the faith could be expected to be dealt with very harshly indeed. While many were imprisoned for their beliefs, it wasn't unusual for those who persisted to be executed in the most horrific way.

Many Catholic believers who felt unable to keep their faith secretly left England for Europe, travelling to places like Italy and France where Catholicism was still the dominant religion. From

The Carnary Chapel is often visited by the ghost of Sir Thomas Erpingham.

time to time, however, some of them would return to England; among them, in 1610, was Revd Thomas Tunstall.

Tunstall was a devout Catholic who felt it his duty to preach the virtues of Catholicism wherever and whenever he could. Finding his way to East Anglia, Tunstall soon set about preaching his beliefs outside the cathedral, which quickly brought him to the attention of the authorities. He was arrested and taken before the Bishop of Norwich. He was accused of blasphemy and, having quickly been found guilty, was sentenced to remain in prison until he changed his ways.

Over the next five years, Tunstall was moved from prison to prison around the area until, in 1615, he found himself in Wisbech prison. From here, he managed to escape by tying his sheets together and lowering himself out of an open window. During his escape, he badly cut and burnt the palms of his hands and he went to a friend's house in Lynn seeking medical attention.

His friend told him there was a lady living nearby who was trained in the art of first aid and offered to take him to see her. The lady in question was Lady l'Estrange, who had a reputation for being a charitable person who would often help the poor and needy. Arriving at her house, Tunstall offered up his hands for inspection and Lady l'Estrange invited him in. After bathing and bandaging his hands, she sent him away, telling him to return the following day for more treatment.

An unsuspecting woman, that night Lady l'Estrange told her husband of her new patient. Her husband, Sir Hamon l'Estrange, was a local Justice of the Peace and immediately realised who his wife's new patient was. He told his wife that her patient was the escaped priest and that he must be seized without delay. Horrified by what had happened, Lady l'Estrange fell to her knees and begged her husband to forget everything she had told him. She claimed she would be unhappy for the rest of her life if the priest should suffer because of her.

Sir Hamon, however, was adamant that the priest should be recaptured and brought to justice, and ignored his wife's pleas for mercy. The following day, when Thomas Tunstall returned to have his hands retreated, Sir Hamon and his army were lying in wait for him. He was quickly rearrested and taken back to Norwich, where he was once again brought before the Bishop. This time he was tried for high treason and, having been found guilty, was sentenced to be hung, drawn and quartered.

Tunstall spent the next few days in the cells at the city's Guildhall. He was imprisoned in a soulless place underground with just a small window for air and he was chained to the wall and given the barest of provisions to live on. Finally, he was taken to the Magdalen Gates, which stood on the perimeter of the city wall. A crowd had gathered to see the execution and, while Thomas Tunstall stood awaiting his fate, Sir Hamon arrived on horseback.

Dismounting from his horse, Sir Hamon made his way to the priest to mock him, saying, 'Well, Mr Tunstall, I find then you are determined to die, and I hope you are prepared for it.' 'Indeed, Sir Hamon,' replied the priest, 'die I must, and I beseech God that my guiltless blood may not lie heavy upon you and yours.' With a cursory bow, Sir Hamon walked back to his horse, remounted and rode away.

A few minutes later, in front of a baying crowd, Thomas Tunstall was hanged from the gates. While Tunstall was hanging and still alive, the executioner took a large knife and plunged it into the priest's stomach, removing his entrails to a great cheer from the crowd. His body was then cut down and the final indignity followed. His head was removed from his shoulders and then his body was cut into four quarters. The head was placed atop the gates in St Benedict's and the four quarters on four different gates. Justice, 1615 style, had been completed.

One hundred and twenty years later, a young man checked into his hotel room at the Maid's Head Hotel. He noticed a painting on the wall, a portrait of a man, not in a frame but actually painted on the wall. For some reason, this portrait disturbed him and he found it difficult to sleep that night. In the morning, he asked the landlord who the portrait was of but the landlord had to admit that he didn't know, it had been there a lot longer than he had. He did tell the young man, however, that several of his guests had complained of it and he was in two minds as to whether to paint over the top of it or not. When the young man returned to the hotel that evening, the landlord told him he had been able to move him to a different room and the young man enjoyed a good night's sleep.

A few days later, on the evening before the young man was due to leave Norwich, he was walking through Tombland on the opposite side of the road to the cathedral. Glancing over towards the impressive building, he saw a figure standing underneath Erpingham Gate. For some reason, the young man felt he knew this figure and crossed the road to see who it was.

As he got closer, he saw that the figure was a man with a most unusual face. It was red and the eyes seemed to be exploding from their sockets, and the veins stood out on his forehead. Looking closer, the young man saw the reason why: this man had a noose tightly knotted around his neck. Glancing down, he saw that the man also had a knife sticking out from his stomach and his entrails were hanging over his belt. Fixing his stare once more on the man's face, he realised why he recognised him: it was the same man whose portrait had been on the wall of his original bedroom at the Maid's Head Hotel. At this point, the character groaned, turned and disappeared into Cathedral Close and the young man raced back to the hotel as quickly as he could.

Recounting his story to the landlord, he realised that the man had been dressed in ecclesiastical clothing that resembled those which would have been worn by a priest. By this time in history, Catholics had been allowed to return to England and many priests now preached throughout the diocese of Norwich. The landlord told the young man that there was a Romish priest who lived on the outskirts of the city who had a book containing portraits of all the priests who had ever preached in the city.

The following morning, the young man went to the priest's church just as early morning Mass was finishing. The priest confirmed that he had a book of portraits and invited the young man to accompany him upstairs to look through it. After a few minutes of turning over the pages, the young man came to a portrait of the character he had seen underneath Erpingham Gate. It was the same man whose portrait had been on his bedroom wall. The portrait was of Thomas Tunstall, the priest hung, drawn and quartered 120 years earlier around 300 yards down the road from Erpingham Gate.

Oliver Cromwell's horses

Few people present at the banquet held in honour of Queen Elizabeth I at the Maid's Head in 1578 would have guessed that less than seventy years later the hotel would be playing host to the forces of another historical leader. Even fewer would have guessed that this man would be committed to, and successful in, overthrowing the monarchy so regally represented by their guest of honour that evening.

Nevertheless, by 1644 all this and more had come true. Following an open conflict with his government, King Charles I had been overthrown by the new force known as the Republicans. The King's supporters, the Cavaliers, had been all but defeated by the Republican forces under the command of Oliver Cromwell. King Charles was imprisoned and Cromwell was more or less running the country on a day-to-day basis.

Erpingham Gate, where the ghost of Revd Tunstall was seen 120 years after his death.

The cathedral was ransacked by Oliver Cromwell's army after their colleagues had been decapitated.

However, small pockets of resistance loyal to the King still existed, among them a group based in Norwich. When news reached London that this group was plotting to free Charles and reinstate him as King of England, Cromwell knew he had to act swiftly and decisively. It was January 1644, the civil war had been practically won by the Republicans and the last thing Cromwell needed was a new group of agitators causing him problems. An army was sent to Norwich to arrest the ringleaders and take them back to London.

When Cromwell's army reached the gates at the top of St Stephens Street, they demanded to be told where the group of conspirators were. Upon being informed that the group were currently feasting at the Maid's Head Hotel, they made their way towards their quarry. Little could they have expected what awaited them. The events of that evening are shrouded in mystery but, for certain, things didn't go the way Cromwell's forces had imagined.

Legend has it that when the army arrived at the Maid's Head Hotel they were told that the conspirators had escaped. People who live in Norwich are well aware of the rumours that abound regarding the tunnels supposed to criss-cross our city below the ground. Tunnels are believed to run as far as from the cathedral to the Guildhall and from the Guildhall to the castle. Certainly there used to be tunnels which ran from the Maid's Head Hotel to the cathedral. These tunnels were used by the monks as they made their secret visits to the inn for an evening tipple. The tunnels were 8-10ft high and 6-8ft across, making it easy for the monks to stagger back to their beds when they had had enough of the inn's hospitality.

Cromwell's army were told that the conspirators had escaped through these tunnels and, still on horseback, they set off in pursuit. What they weren't expecting, however, was that the conspirators had secreted themselves in alcoves along the tunnels and had laid lengths of steel rope across the floor. As Cromwell's army raced down the tunnels, they raced to their deaths. Waiting until just the right moment, the conspirators suddenly pulled up their lengths of steel rope, decapitating both the horses and their riders upon them.

What we do know is that, a few days later, a second army sent by Cromwell arrived in the city. This second army attacked the cathedral, causing untold damage. The giant wooden doors were ripped from their hinges and taken to the marketplace, where they were set alight. Anything that could be moved was dragged from the building and added to the giant bonfire now burning in the marketplace. Windows and doors were smashed, monks were assaulted and Bishop Hall was forced to flee and take refuge at the Bishop's Palace in Heigham Street, now the Dolphin public house.

The destruction was overwhelming and shocked the city. More damage was inflicted upon the cathedral than on any other ecclesiastical building during the entire English Civil War. Nobody could work out why Oliver Cromwell was so angry.

Maybe we can guess at the cause of his anger. Maybe it was because, less than seventy-two hours earlier, his first army had been slaughtered as they raced through the tunnels below the cathedral grounds. And maybe that's also why, if you wander about the grounds around midnight towards the end of January, you will hear the sound of horses racing, not above the ground but below it. Horses without their riders and, quite likely, without their heads.

The Phantom Room

In the basement of the offices of solicitors Leathes Prior is a room that has always been referred to as the Phantom Room. Where or when the name originates from, no one is sure. However, in 1997, the room really lived up to its name.

When builders were called in to remove a stone-clad staircase in the basement, they seemed to disturb more than just the old brickwork. In a room several floors above the basement, staff looked on in astonishment as paper clips and a hole-punch started to jump up and down on a desk. Later, a calendar began swinging like a pendulum and a clock began to move of its own accord and ended up hanging at an angle which defied gravity.

Each occurrence was accompanied by the room becoming very cold and a fusty smell in the air. Staff claimed they could sense a horrible presence in the room. When a cupboard door began to open and close rapidly, banging against a desk, they decided it was time to take action and called in a Church of England deliverance team. A few days later, the room was exorcised and calm returned to the offices. The builders, who had reported feeling uneasy while working in the basement, also claimed that the feeling of being watched had gone. It's still called the Phantom Room but it seems the phantom has now well and truly gone.

The Phantom Room lies in the basement of the offices of Leathes Prior.

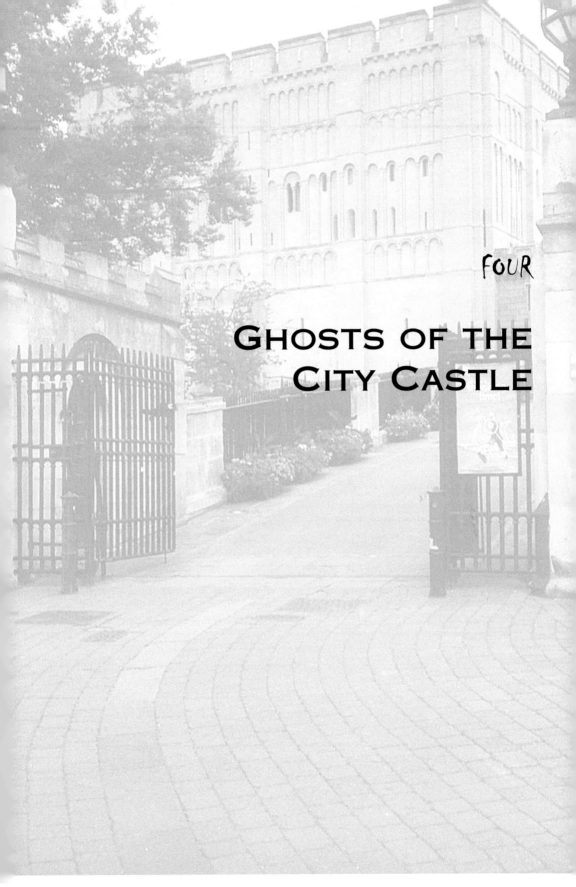

FOUR

GHOSTS OF THE
CITY CASTLE

Having stood proudly on its mound overlooking the city for almost 1,000 years, it should come as no surprise that the city castle has a wonderful story to tell. Home to the Normans and subjected to many battles and sieges, the castle soon became a place of trial, torture and execution. It was the site of the burning of witches and religious dissenters, the pressing and racking of convicted villains and the hanging of felons – both inside and outside and even, in the case of Robert Kett, from the battlements. It was the location of a court, a gaol and finally a museum. Little wonder, then, that it has a tale or two to tell.

Many different ghosts claim to have been seen over the years but the most popular appear to be a floating skull, an old Victorian lady and a young lad. There are others, of course, including the old man in a raincoat who may have just been somebody locked in one night.

The floating skull appears to be a head that is seen around the keep area from time to time. Those who have seen it claim that it suddenly materialises from nowhere, floats for a few moments and then disappears as quickly as it came. There are several theories about who the skull might have originally belonged to but the most likely would seem to be Robert Goodale, who was hanged at the castle in 1885. We'll examine the case of Mr Goodale in more detail later.

The Victorian lady is a little more subtle. Usually spotted around the art exhibition area, she is often seen walking along, admiring the paintings on the walls. Always dressed from head to toe in long, flowing, black Victorian clothes, she wanders up and down the corridors, talking to no one. Those who have followed her claim that she suddenly turns a corner and then is no longer to be seen, as if she has simply disappeared into one of the paintings she has been admiring. There are no obvious candidates for who this old lady may have been. She appears too well dressed to be one of the many female prisoners who were held here during the Victorian age, when the castle was used as a prison, and there are no other records held which give a clue to her identity.

The young lad often seen around the dungeon area may be a little easier to identify. The most likely candidate is Robert Cooper, who was held at the castle in 1898. As part of his punishment, he was set to work on the treadmill and when he complained of feeling ill and being unable to work it was assumed he was merely shirking. His bed was taken away from him and he was made to sleep on the bare floor. The guards continued to make him work on the treadmill for many days after he first claimed to be unwell. One morning when they entered his cell, they found him dead on the floor; it seems that he had died from exhaustion. Many people believe it is the ghost of Robert who still wanders around the dungeons and the area where the cells used to stand.

Those are the main ghosts of the castle but probably just as famous are the two Egyptian mummies which stand on the top floor. Who hasn't met somebody who claims that the eyes have moved from side to side while they have been watching them?

Executions at the castle could be carried out in a number of ways. As we've already seen, witches and Lollards were often burnt alive while, during the years of the plagues, offenders would often be dropped to their death. Justice could be swift, as in the case of beheading, or take a matter of days to complete. One novel way of executing a person was to 'press' them to death. This process could be long and drawn out and would take many days to complete. A prisoner sentenced to pressing would be laid on a stone bed and then have heavy weights placed upon his body. Each day, he would be given a little water to drink and then further weights would be added to those already on him until life was literally pressed out of him. The most common form of execution, however, was that of hanging. In extreme cases, an unlucky victim could be subject to more than one form of execution: in July 1639, a prisoner named John Botolph was hanged at the castle 'for running away after prest'.

The castle keep, where a floating skull is often seen.

On occasion, judges would decide that hanging was too severe a penalty to impose for a certain crime and take a more lenient stance, although there may have been some offenders who would question the leniency of some of these sentences. Hard labour, which could mean anything from picking oakum to working on the treadmill, would often be imposed, but sometimes hard labour would be only one part of the punishment handed out by the courts. At the April 1787 Lent Assizes, Joseph Marden, a chimney sweep, was convicted of stealing an ass. His punishment came in three parts: first, he was to be publicly whipped on Castle Hill, then the second part of his punishment was to serve six months' hard labour at Wymondham Bridewell. He must have completed the six months with a heavy heart, as the third part of his punishment was that at the end of his hard labour he was to be publicly whipped again.

Whipping formed a regular part of the punishments handed out by the local courts. In April 1875, twenty-five-year-old William Sillis, a local labourer, was found guilty of assaulting Miss Ann Elizabeth Blyth at Great Massingham the previous October. He was sentenced to eighteen years' penal servitude which would start with twenty lashes of the 'cat'. The punishment took place at the castle on 20 April 1875. Sillis was tied to the whipping post by his hands and feet and his back was bared. The whipping was carried out by the prison governor, a Mr Pinson, and the 'cat' consisted of nine tails of braided whipcord. After the third lash had been administered, Sillis turned his head and pleaded, 'For God's sake, don't hit twice in the same place.' Unmoved, Pinson carried on the whipping, ignoring the howling and wincing of the prisoner, who appeared to break down completely after the eighth lash. Undeterred by the sight of a semi-conscious man in front of him, Pinson continued for another twelve lashes, finishing the session dripping with sweat and breathing heavily. After being cut down, Sillis was dragged away, muttering to a turnkey that, 'a poor devil had better be hanged than punished like that.'

Sex and age appear to have had little influence on the use of the whip. Many women were whipped privately for various offences and often youths regarded as no more than children would find themselves tied to the whipping post. Two of the youngest people known to have been whipped were fourteen-year-old Alfred Thirkettle and his partner in crime, thirteen-year-old Thomas Browne. Both had been convicted of theft at the 1834 Lent Assizes. Their haul had consisted of two thermometers, an ivory figure and a china ornament.

At the same assizes, in a macabre display of keeping it in the family, Thirkettle's uncle, William, had been found guilty of intent to murder his wife Maria. A few days later, with his back still raw from the whipping, Alfred saw his uncle hanged in front of the castle. Those who had hoped that such a sight might have a redeeming influence on the young Thirkettle were to be sadly disappointed. At the very next General Quarter Sessions, in October, Alfred was back in the dock, accused of stealing clothing and money from Robert Wright. He had, in fact, been arrested and held in the castle since August, a mere four months after his whipping. Having been found guilty, Thirkettle was sentenced to fourteen years' transportation to Australia, from where he was never to return.

The pillory was often used as an instrument of punishment and torture. Offenders would be placed in the pillory or stocks for up to a week, during which time the general public would be invited to throw rotten fruit, rotten vegetables, bad eggs and other forms of rubbish at them.

During the reign of Queen Elizabeth I, an unfortunate man by the name of James Gold was overheard to say something uncomplimentary about the Queen and her religious beliefs. A bailiff nearby promptly arrested him and he was taken to the castle and placed in the dungeons. Word was sent to Her Majesty and she deemed that the poor man should spend a week in the

The Castle Ditches, where many witches and Lollards met their deaths.

pillory without food or drink. As if this wasn't enough, she instructed that his ears should be nailed to the pillory for the entire week.

At the end of the week, he was released and taken out but, as he couldn't afford to pay his fine, he was then promptly burnt alive in the Castle Ditches. Could this James Gold be the young man who used to be seen wandering around the ditches with nails through his ears long before the punk movement began?

By 1803, burnings were no longer taking place but the pillory was still often used as a punishment. In June, two lads named Denny and Allen were found guilty of conspiracy. Both had blamed the other for the crime and it was decided that they would both stand for one hour in the pillory in the marketplace.

Allen wept bitterly as he was placed under the wooden beam but Denny treated it all very much as a joke. Laughing and smiling, he winked and nodded at the crowd as they gathered to watch the spectacle. Finally, he began to pull faces at the crowd and, incensed by his behaviour, the crowd responded by throwing eggs at him. Still Denny continued to smile and laugh until finally the crowd began to shower him with potatoes. At this point, the smile quickly left Denny's face and after half an hour or so of being hit by the potatoes he finally passed out. Denny was removed from the pillory and taken to the Guildhall, where he was examined by several medical men. After a brief examination, it was decided that he was fit enough to continue with his punishment and he was returned to the pillory, where he spent another half an hour facing the eggs and potatoes.

At the end of the required hour, during which Allen had been left virtually unscathed, both men were removed and taken to the Bridewell where they were placed in solitary confinement for two years. Long enough, no doubt, to wipe the smile off Denny's face for good!

The hangings

Hangings, however, remained the most popular form of punishment and these were a regular feature of city life in the 1800s. Many of the city's criminals were hanged outside the castle. A platform would be set up between the two gatehouses, the gallows would be put on top with a trapdoor underneath and then the convicted person would be brought out to meet their end. These proceedings weren't carried out in private or kept quiet. On the contrary, huge bill posters

Many criminals were hanged between the gatehouses of the castle.

inviting people to attend would be placed around the city. Often, whole families would come laden with picnic baskets for a day out.

When James Bloomfield Rush was hanged in April 1849 for shooting dead the Recorder of Norwich and his son, special transport had to be laid on to bring in all the people who wanted to witness the end of Mr Rush. Trains ran from Wymondham, Dereham, Fakenham, Ipswich, Lowestoft and Yarmouth as the county came to watch the execution. It was reported that a crowd in excess of 20,000 people came to view the event.

An even larger crowd was recorded in April 1779, when five highway robbers were hanged all at the same time. The hangings coincided with the Easter fair so there would have been a funfair in the background. Children would have been enjoying the rides and walking around with candyfloss or toffee apples as their parents fought for the best view on the mound. It was recorded that a crowd in excess of 30,000 people attended that day. The local paper revealed that many pockets had been picked on the day and, a few months later, some of those who had been caught pickpocketing met the same fate as the highway robbers had that day. Twenty-two years later, the first national census revealed that Norwich had a population of 47,313, showing that almost three-quarters of the entire population had attended the hangings that day.

The families of the hanged criminals were often left destitute after the sentence had been carried out. There was no such thing as state benefits and many wives and children were left to beg on the streets to survive. Being caught doing this could also carry the punishment of whipping. One or two, however, came up with more ingenious methods of making money.

Following the hanging of her husband in 1831 for setting fire to haystacks, a Mrs Nockolds applied to be allowed to take his body away for a private burial. Her wish was granted and she promptly wheeled the body of her late husband on a barrow back to her cottage on the outskirts of the city. There she displayed it in the front room, charging the curious a penny each to view it. A considerable amount of money was raised; indeed, she was heard to claim that she had got more from her late husband dead than she ever did when he was alive. Finally, the body began to decompose and she was ordered by the authorities to have it buried.

Four years later, in 1835, James Clarke was also hanged for setting fire to a wheat stack. At his execution, an old man named Wyer, a person well known for his eccentricities, declared on the Hill that he would take the young man's place for the sum of five shillings. Somebody paid him the money in an attempt to shut him up and the old man went home and promptly kept his word by hanging himself from the staircase.

But possibly the most unnerving start to any hanging came in 1822, when James Smith and Henry Clarke were due to be hanged together for breaking and entering. The cart carrying them from the city gaol suffered a broken wheel on its way to the castle and so they were transferred to a second cart for the remainder of their journey. With their arms tied behind them, the two men made their way to the castle sitting on black cloths in the cart, unaware that they were in fact sitting on top of the very coffins in which their bodies would be taken back to the gaol.

In the 1860s, mainly due to the unruly behaviour that was now common place at these events, it was decided that public hangings were no longer acceptable and in future convicted criminals would be hanged in private. The first person to be privately hanged was William Sheward, who had murdered his wife as long ago as 1851 but was only brought to justice some eighteen years later, following his long overdue confession. Sheward was the last person to be hanged at the old city gaol.

It was at a hanging inside the castle that one of the city's most notorious incidents took place. In the November sessions of 1885, Robert Goodale had been found guilty of murdering his wife the previous September. After the murder, he had dumped his wife's body in a local well, where it had been found a few days later. At first, Goodale claimed his wife must have fallen in.

When the strangulation marks on her neck were pointed out, he suggested that maybe some nettles had wrapped themselves around her neck as she fell down the well. Having been found guilty, Goodale was taken to the castle to await his execution.

Prior to a hanging, the executioner would take a general look at the convicted prisoner to determine his size and weight. This was to allow him to make the correct calculations as to what the drop should be. The drop is the length of rope that is loose when the convicted felon is standing on the trapdoor. If the executioner got the measurement wrong, the hanged man could end up being strangled to death as opposed to having his neck broken. There are several recorded instances where the drop has been wrong and there have been people hiding beneath the scaffold to pull down on the legs of the criminals who have just been hanged and finish the job off.

Robert Goodale was a big man, judged to be around 6ft tall and weighing some 15-16 stone, and it would seem that on this occasion the hangman got the drop dreadfully wrong, with appalling consequences. On the morning of the execution, the scaffold was tested with a weight of 16 stone and appeared to be working perfectly. However, just one hour later, as Goodale stood on the trapdoor and Berry, the executioner, pulled the bolt, something went dreadfully wrong. Goodale fell through the trapdoor easily enough but then the noose reappeared without him. Initially, it was thought that the rope had come off his head and that Goodale, with arms tied behind his back and legs pinioned together, had fallen the 10ft or so into the concrete pit. The thought that he may have suffered broken arms or legs filled the execution team with horror, as they knew they would have to carry him back to the scaffold and hang him again while he was in extreme pain.

However, their horror turned to disbelief when they peered through the trapdoor to see the dead body of Goodale lying on one side of the pit. On the other side of the pit lay his head, still covered with the hood that he had been wearing when the trapdoor opened but now totally separated from his body. At the subsequent inquest, Berry told the jury that Goodale's head had come off 'as if cut by a knife'.

Maybe the story of Robert Goodale answers the question of the identity of the floating skull in the castle keep. It is hard to think of a more likely candidate for the role.

FIVE

Haunted Pubs

The Lamb Inn

One of the most popular hangings ever to take place at the city castle was that of Timothy Hardy, who had murdered a local publican in 1757. The pub where the murder took place has recently reopened as Henry's Bar. For the past few years it has been known as the Rat and Parrot but in 1757, when John Aggas was the landlord, it was known – as it still is to most people in the city today – as the Lamb Inn.

John Aggas was a large fifty-one-year-old man with a personality to match his size. A great lover of storytelling, he would spend all day telling stories to his children. Stories about fairies and goblins, pixies and elves, stories we don't tell anymore today. So popular were John's stories that people would come from far and wide to bring their children to hear them. Even other landlords would come along with their families to hear his latest tale of adventure.

Aggas had a brother-in-law, a man by the name of Timothy Hardy, who was not such an amenable fellow at all. Hardy had a reputation of always being on the edge of trouble and always spoiling for a fight. When John Aggas's sister had married Hardy, Aggas remarked that it wouldn't be long before there was trouble. Little did he realise that his prediction would come true so tragically.

Hardy lived with his wife in Newton Flotman, on the outskirts of the city. On Saturday 10 November 1797, they made their way on foot into Norwich. When they got about halfway, Hardy suddenly stopped and claimed he had to return home as he had left his knife behind. His wife said that it wasn't important but Hardy replied that if he didn't have it on him he would be damned and he insisted on returning for it. However, he then discovered that the knife was in fact in his pocket and they carried on making their way into the city.

Later that afternoon, Hardy and his wife went to the Lamb Inn, where they made their way downstairs to the kitchen. After a few minutes, an argument between them broke out and Hardy began to push his wife around. Hearing the commotion, John Aggas went into the kitchen to try and cool the situation. Hardy stopped shouting and, in what appeared to be an act of friendship, he turned around and offered his hand to Aggas, claiming that he did not wish to argue with him although he disagreed with his sister. However, as John Aggas stepped forward to take Hardy's hand, Hardy pulled out his knife, plunged it deep into Aggas's stomach and ripped up his belly for about 3-4in, causing a large portion of his bowels to fall out.

There were several witnesses present at the time who claimed that, once the stabbing was over, Hardy shouted, 'I have done for you and were my brother, John Hardy of Lynn, here I would serve him the same. And now I'll stab myself for I know I must die for it.' At this point, Hardy made a feeble attempt to stab himself, causing only superficial injuries; he was then overpowered by the others present in the kitchen. He was held until the police and a doctor arrived.

Despite the best efforts of the doctor, John Aggas died the following morning. Hardy was taken to the castle, where he stayed until the Summer Assizes the following year. At the assizes he was sentenced to hang and his body be dissected.

Following his death, the family of John Aggas sold the Lamb Inn and moved away. They claimed the inn held too many bad memories for them and they moved to the other side of the city. However, it seems that John Aggas himself was far from ready to move on. Almost as soon as the new landlord moved in, unexplained happenings began and they have been continuing ever since.

Every landlord in living memory will tell you of the lonely footsteps that can be heard walking up and down the corridors at night, when there is nobody to be seen. Late night knocks on bedroom doors are often heard but there is nobody standing on the other side, no matter how quickly the doors are opened. In the kitchen, the scene of the murder, unwashed cutlery left overnight is often found washed and put away in the morning.

Perhaps it is the children of the landlords that we should listen to most. For almost every child of every landlord will tell the same story, of how they have woken in the night to find an old man sitting at the foot of their beds. Surprisingly, none of the children have ever claimed to have been scared by the elderly apparition, who then goes on to tell them the most wonderful stories. Stories of fairies and goblins, pixies and elves, stories that date back through the centuries, stories that we don't tell anymore today. To this very day, people will go into the inn and ask the landlord, 'Who's the old man telling the stories in the courtyard?' And yet, when the landlord comes out to investigate, the old man has always disappeared.

During the 1980s, the Lamb Inn was used on a regular basis by a market research company. Young girls would bring suitable candidates upstairs to ask them various questions on the latest

The Lamb Inn, home to the ghost of John Aggas.

cosmetics or drinks that were on sale. One day, when there were two young girls conducting their research upstairs, an elderly gentleman came up the stairs. He nodded and smiled at the two women, walked past their desks and left via a door at the far end of the room. The young girls took little notice, assuming it was somebody who worked there. Some time later, it was time for them to leave and, as the old man hadn't reappeared, they decided they would tell him they were going. Imagine their surprise when they opened the door to find themselves looking into an empty cupboard. A little research found that the doorway once led to another part of the inn, which would have been there during the time of John Aggas's tenancy. Was it just John making his way from one side of the inn to the other?

The most recent sighting of Aggas came in 1999, after a relief manager had locked the inn and gone upstairs to have something to eat with his girlfriend. Quickly checking the security monitor, he spotted an elderly gentleman sitting in a chair by the window. Believing he had locked somebody in, he told his girlfriend he was going back downstairs to let him out. However, once in the bar downstairs he found the seat empty and, despite a thorough search of the inn, the old man appeared to have disappeared. Surprisingly, every door and window remained locked from the inside and so there was no way he could have left.

The manager returned upstairs to recheck the video recording on the monitor but, when he got back to the point where he had seen the old man, the monitor recording showed only an empty chair. It would appear that despite his willingness to tell stories, John Aggas remains camera shy.

The Wild Man

The Wild Man pub stands at the top of London Street, opposite the impressive National Westminster Bank. Back in the 1800s, the building was used as an overflow for the prison when all their cells were full. It would appear that it is from those days that the ghost of the Wild Man originates.

Strictly speaking, the pub should be called the Wild Boy. Even today, its pub sign shows a young male child and until around twenty years ago the sign was even more vivid, as it depicted a young boy behind bars surrounded by flames. That sign used to give a clue to the ghost who is reputed to live downstairs.

Back in the late 1800s, there were several families of gypsies living on Mousehold Heath on the outskirts of the city. One day, a young lad from the camp came into the city and stole a loaf of bread. He was very unlucky for two reasons. The first reason was that he got caught and the second reason was that the Summer Assizes were in session that very day at the city castle. The traders who had caught him marched him to the castle and he was dragged before the judge the very same afternoon and tried for stealing, found guilty and sentenced to hang at the weekend.

These were the 'good old days' of Norwich that our grandparents remind us of from time to time, days like the one in 1837 when eighteen men were sentenced to hang in one afternoon. Of the eighteen, one had committed a murder, others had stolen horses or sheep – usually to feed their families – some had set fire to haystacks and one of them, a young lad of sixteen, had stolen his master's silk handkerchief. This boy stole a handkerchief, was thrown into the dungeons for around nine months until the judge next came to the city and was then sentenced to hang. 'Good old days' indeed!

Back to our Wild Boy. As all the cells in the castle were full, he was brought back to what is now the Wild Man pub and taken downstairs to the cells below. It was a tradition that anyone sentenced to hang would not be dealt with until after the judge who had sentenced them had

The Wild Man pub, where the Wild Boy still roams.

left the city. Accordingly, the young gypsy boy would remain in the cells until the weekend, when he would meet his fate.

His family of gypsies on Mousehold Heath heard what had happened to him and decided they would try to rescue him. So that night, under the cover of darkness, they came into the city and tried to break down the doors behind which their young companion was being held. Despite their efforts, they could not force open the doors and they desperately tried to think of another way to save the young boy. Finally, they came up with a plan. They decided as they couldn't break their way in they would burn their way in instead and they set fire to the doors.

Unfortunately, the plan backfired. The entire building became engulfed in flames and, far from saving the young lad, they actually robbed him of the last few days of his life, as he burnt to death in the cells downstairs. Ever since then, it has been claimed that the Wild Man is haunted by the ghost of the Wild Boy.

If you should ever venture into the cellars of the Wild Man pub, you will find that they are exceptionally cold. All pub cellars are meant to be cold for obvious reasons but the Wild Man has the coldest cellars in the city. It is believed that it is the Wild Boy who keeps them so cold, so that the heat of the flames won't burn him to death a second time. Also, if you talk to the landlords, they will tell you of the tables and chairs that get moved around at night and the picture that gets turned round to face the wall.

In the 1970s, the landlord of the Wild Man was a man called Keith. One night after the bar had closed, Keith and his wife Sandy were upstairs watching television when they heard the noise of something being moved in the cellar. Keith went down to investigate and, when he got there, he found a large keg of beer had been moved from one end of the cellar to the other. There was a marked line on the floor were it had been dragged. Keith was a big, strong man and he tried to drag the keg back to where it had come from, but he couldn't move it an inch. The following morning, with the help of his two pot men, he managed to get it back to its original position. Somebody had dragged it in the opposite direction less than twelve hours earlier. Maybe the Wild Boy has grown a few muscles since he was imprisoned.

The Coachmakers' Arms

Situated just outside the old city walls at the top of St Stephens Street, the Coachmakers' Arms stands on the site of an old leper house. Leper houses were fairly common in Norwich and were usually built on the outskirts of the city. The Lazar House on Sprowston Road was such a building, as was the hospital along St Giles Street. However, it is only the site where the Coachmakers' Arms now stands that claims to have a ghostly reminder from those days.

Many barmaids working at the pub have gone to serve a shadowy figure standing at the end of the bar, only to find when they get there that there is no one waiting. The general description of him seems to be a Dick Turpin-style highwayman. Let's not forget that the lepers would have been brought to the house in horse-drawn trucks; could this 'Dick Turpin' fellow simply be one of the coachmen who delivered them?

Our coachman is not the only ghost to be seen around the pub. A lady dressed all in black has often been spotted coming down the stairs. Some members of staff have thought that this might be one of the old lepers but this is most unlikely. The lepers would have almost certainly have been dressed in grey or dirty white rags. The well-dressed lady is far more likely to be an ex-member of staff who looked after the lepers at the house. Maybe she comes down to share a drink with her 'highwayman' and talk about old times.

The ghosts at the pub are known to be a little boisterous at times and many members of staff have witnessed bottles and glasses falling over, as well as the occasional painting falling from the wall. Some may say it's simply the result of a strong wind from time to time, but it's just as likely to be the unseen hand of one of the old lepers.

The Coachmakers' Arms, which is still visited by inmates of the old Leper House.

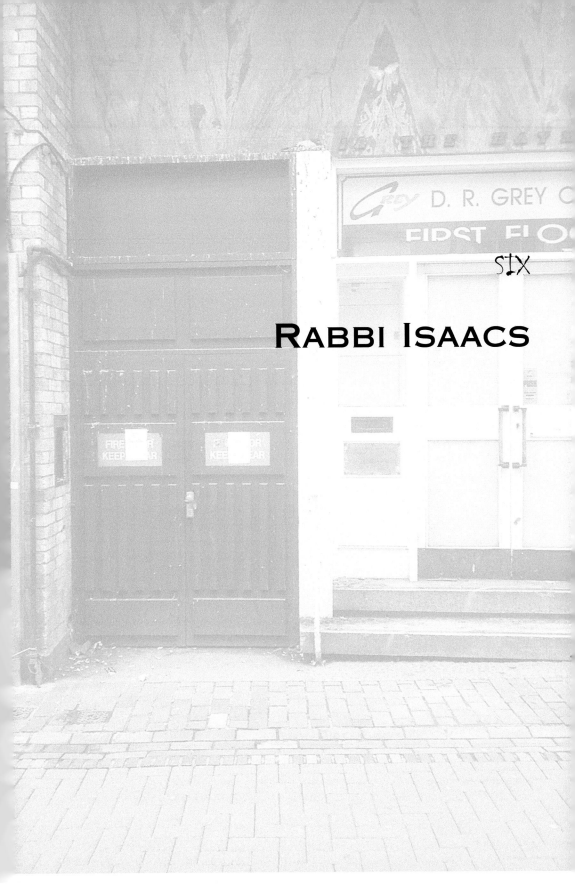

SIX

RABBI ISAACS

White Lion Street runs just off the marketplace and, along with Back of the Inns and Gentleman's Walk, in the 1100s formed the main area inhabited by the local Jews. It's where they lived, where they worked and where they played and, perhaps most important of all, where they prayed. Their synagogue was built halfway along White Lion Street and stretched right through to Gentleman's Walk. It was believed at the time that the cellars below the synagogue were the largest in England and it was the place where many of the local Jewry spent many nights debating their beliefs.

The rabbi in charge of the synagogue was a man by the name of Isaacs. Rabbi Isaacs was married. His faith allowed him to be married but he doesn't seem to have made a very fortuitous choice for his partner. The rabbi was married to a very domineering woman, whose word appeared to be law in the Isaacs household. Isaacs did everything his wife told him and took on the role of a henpecked husband for all to see.

When told by his wife to jump, he would simply ask 'How high?'. When told to shut up, he would ask 'For how long?' He was well and truly under his wife's thumb. Feared by many who met her, Rabbi Isaacs' wife gained a reputation for being a most unpleasant woman and there was little sorrow expressed when she appeared to go missing one day. However, when the rabbi failed to come up with any convincing explanations as to where she had gone, many rumours began to spread, including one that maybe he had killed her.

These rumours were swiftly forgotten at Easter 1144, when the Jewish community suddenly found itself under attack from the local citizens. A young local boy named William was found dead in Thorpe Wood. It appeared he had been crucified and suspicion fell upon the Jews. An angry mob gathered and demanded that the Jews be tried for the murder. The Jews, however, were seen as the King's men and were under the protection of the sheriff and therefore no charges were brought against them.

Some weeks later, the locals decided to invoke their own justice and a terrible persecution of the Jews began. All were chased from their homes to the outskirts of the city and threatened with death should they return. A systematic destruction then began on their buildings, houses and shops. Even the synagogue was reduced to rubble, leaving the White Lion Street area little more than a pile of old bricks and twisted wood.

Many years later, in 1501, work started on a new building on the site of the old synagogue. The building was to become known as the Curat House and was built by local merchant and one time mayor John Curat. Over the following centuries, the building was used by many different businesses until it was finally bought by the Backs family. Backs' was a wine merchant's and chandler's before becoming a public house and then a wine bar, finally closing in the 1980s. When it was a chandler's and wine merchant's, it became very popular and successful, so successful that more room was needed to store the stock.

The Backs decided to excavate the old cellars of the synagogue which remained below the building. A long process of removing all the rubble from the 1144 destruction of the synagogue began and the workmen were surprised when they began to find little mementos of the Jewish faith. Small goblets and angels were brought out and then, as the work neared completion, a long wooden box was discovered. When the box was opened, it was found to contain a set of old bones. The bones were sent to London to be examined and, after much deliberation, were declared to be the bones of a woman dating back many centuries, possibly as far back as the 1100s. It is believed that these bones belonged to the wife of Rabbi Isaacs.

Almost immediately, the building acquired a ghost but not the ghost that many might have expected. It wasn't the ghost of the wife of Rabbi Isaacs who began to walk the corridors at night but that of the rabbi himself. Unfortunately, the rabbi is not a particularly friendly ghost; he is one of very few ghosts in the city who appear to look for trouble. The staff who worked at Backs' didn't stay very long. They could be walking down a corridor carrying a tray with cups,

The Curat House, where Rabbi Isaacs wanders at night.

saucers or plates when the rabbi would suddenly appear in front of them and try to knock the tray from their hands. He would trip them up or try to push them down the stairs. He would turn their handbags upside down and tip all the contents on to the floor. On other occasions, he would appear and begin to shout or swear at them. If they shouted back, he would simply walk through a door, and I do mean 'through' – he wouldn't bother to open it first. If they followed him into the next room, of course, the room would always be empty. As I said, the staff didn't stay very long.

Until a few years ago, the building was owned by the clothes shop Next. One of the managers of the shop was a young woman named Paula. Many times when Paula was on duty and it was time to close the shop, she would turn off the lights, go outside and lock the doors and, just as she was about to walk away, the lights would come back on. She would unlock the doors, return into the shop and turn the lights off again. Outside the shop, she would relock the front doors and, just as she was to walk away again, the lights would come back on. So a third time she would go into the shop and turn the lights off. This time she would look around and call out, 'Mr. Isaacs! Will you pack it in!' Returning outside, she would relock the front doors and this time the lights would stay off. Some 850 years later and it still seems the rabbi is under the thumb of a dominant woman.

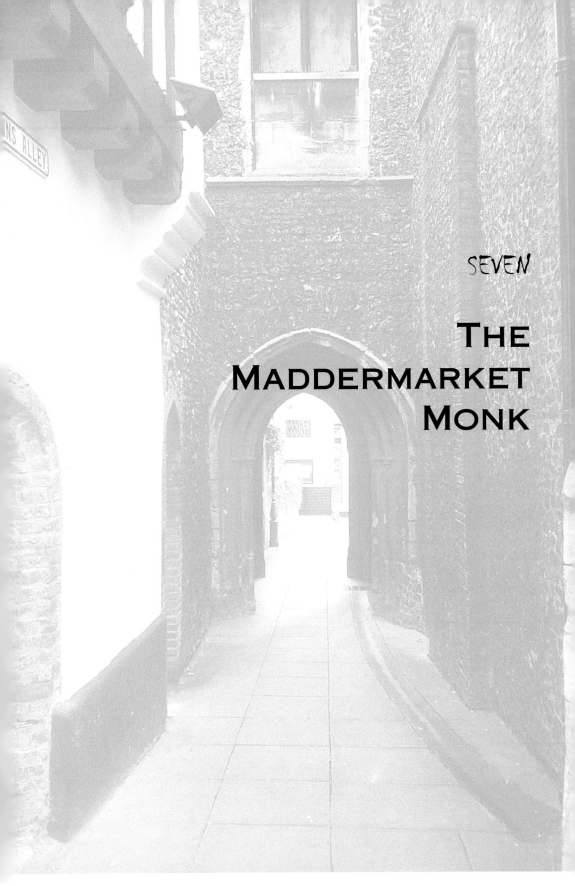

SEVEN

THE MADDERMARKET MONK

Slightly out of the city centre and down a narrow alleyway stands the Maddermarket Theatre. Its name derives from the area on which it was built, originally a madder market selling dyes and cloth to the weavers from the Netherlands who had settled in Norwich.

In 1794, when the market was moved, a Roman Catholic chapel was built on the site. Another, larger church stood at the top of the alleyway and behind the church was a graveyard running down to what is now the main road. The churchyard dates back many centuries and contains what is left of many victims of the various plagues that visited the city. Built on a steep hill, the rainwater runs through the graveyard and comes out at the bottom through a public water pump. No doubt this pump contributed to many upset stomachs in the city.

It is from the chapel that the Maddermarket ghost seems to have originated. In 1921, the chapel was converted into a theatre by Walter Nugent Monck and promptly named the Maddermarket Theatre. Nugent Monck was a founder member of the Norwich Players and recognised that, with its barrel roof copying that of the Sistine Chapel, the acoustics offered by the building would be second to none in the area.

Shortly after the conversion, Nugent Monck was overheard to comment that 'every theatre worthy of its name should have its own ghost' and it wasn't long before the Maddermarket ghost made its first appearance. Perhaps not too surprisingly, as the theatre had originally been a chapel, the ghost turned out to be the ghost of a monk. The monk is reputed to haunt the alleyway that runs between the theatre and the graveyard, the courtyard of the theatre and, of course, the theatre itself.

The first person to see the ghost was Nugent Monck himself. Sitting in the stalls one day watching rehearsals, he saw a monk come out of one of the confessional boxes still standing by the side of the stage. The monk then crossed the stage behind the other actors and went into another confessional box on the opposite side of the stage.

Assuming this was part of the play, Nugent Monck paid little attention to it until all the other actors had left the stage and the monk had not reappeared. Climbing onto the stage, Nugent Monck crossed to the confessional box and opened its door. When he did so, he found himself looking into an empty box. The legend of the monk had begun.

Many actors began to report unusual happenings in the theatre; nothing serious, just the occasional costume being moved or doors becoming jammed from one side. However, as they became more and more regular, some cast members started to make mention of the ghost.

Things became far more serious, however, when the ghost decided to watch a performance one evening. Sitting by the side of the stage, a prompter by the name of Peter Taylor Smith was following the script in case any of the actors forgot their lines. Suddenly, he had an overwhelming desire to turn and look to his right. When he did so, he saw the monk standing on the side of the stage. After a few moments, the monk disappeared but Taylor Smith had lost his concentration and his place in the script. It was unfortunate that one of the actors chose that moment to forget his lines and called desperately for a prompt. Unable to find his place in the script, Taylor Smith was unable to provide the prompt and the play fell into something of a shambles.

It is not too surprising that, when the play was over, Taylor Smith was summoned to the manager's office to explain what had happened. More surprising was the fact that when he got there he found a young couple who had been sitting in the front row of the stalls asking the manager why there had been a monk standing by the side of the stage during the performance.

Some years later, the theatre staged a production of *Murder in the Cathedral*, the play based on the death of Thomas à Becket. During one performance, the actor playing the role of Becket suddenly froze on stage while delivering his eulogy. He stood completely still, neither moving or speaking. Hilda Wells, an actress who had been with the Norwich Players for many years, was on stage at the same time and glanced over towards him to see what the problem was.

As she did so, she noticed a shadow forming behind him and she nudged the young girl on stage next to her to see whether or not she could also see the shadow. The young girl indicated that she could and, as the two women watched, the shadow appeared to take the shape of a monk and gave the actor a cuddle. Upon this happening, the actor immediately continued with his eulogy as if nothing had happened. Later, when Hilda and her co-actress told him of what they had seen, the actor couldn't remember even having paused on stage, let alone having stood

The Maddermarket Theatre, where a mysterious monk takes part in performances.

completely still for the three or four seconds the two women had watched him standing frozen to the spot.

On yet another occasion, a young engineer was climbing up his ladder to the top of the lighting rig when he became aware of somebody climbing the ladder in front of him. When he got to the top, there was nobody else there. Many other actors, engineers and audience members have heard or witnessed the monk as he makes his way around the theatre.

The most recent occurrence was in September 2004, when the cast were performing a dress rehearsal for Oscar Wilde's *Lady Windermere's Fan*. Suddenly, one of the young actresses seemed to jump back from the front of the stage. As she did so, a light fitting crashed to the floor where she had been standing seconds earlier. Other members of the cast crowded round her to check she was all right. Someone commented on how lucky she had been to see the fitting coming and jump back just in time. The young actress was quite adamant that she hadn't jumped at all, somebody had pushed her.

The most mysterious sighting of the monk came during a performance of the play *Agnes of God*. A party of thirty schoolchildren had been brought to one of the performances. These children were aged nine, ten and eleven years old. The following day at school their teachers asked them to write an essay about what they thought of the play, what they liked, what they didn't like, what was good, what was bad, what their favourite moments were and so on. Out of the thirty schoolchildren, fourteen of them wrote that their favourite moment had been when a monk had walked across the stage and made a suspended crucifix turn round without touching it. No wonder the teachers were surprised – there is no monk in *Agnes of God*.

As Nugent Monck himself said, 'every theatre worthy of its name should have its own ghost'. It would seem that the Maddermarket has one of the best ghosts of any theatre. Next time you are there watching a performance, keep one eye open for that shadowy character wandering around.

The Maddermarket Monk still walks up and down this alleyway.

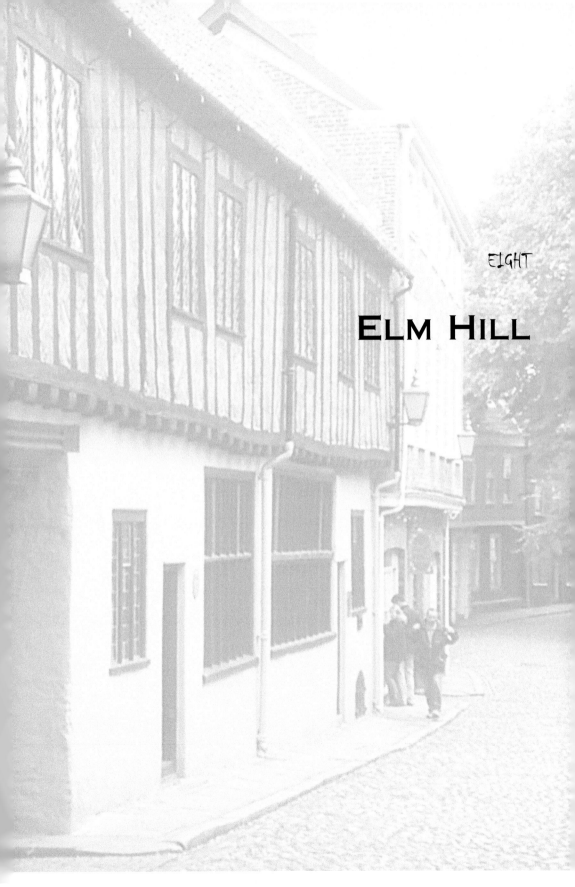

EIGHT

Elm Hill

One of the oldest streets in the city is Elm Hill. The street was largely rebuilt after the great fire of 1507, so many of the buildings are genuine Tudor houses. It is regularly claimed by local guides that there are in fact more Tudor houses in Elm Hill than there are in the whole of London. This claim sounds less impressive when you realise that the Great Fire of 1666 left just one Tudor house standing in the capital. Nonetheless, Elm Hill is a splendid example of a Tudor street in all its glory. But behind the beauty of the Hill lies a story of death, horror and religious fervour.

When the great fire broke out in 1507, a family living in the top half of a house on the left-hand side of the street were trapped by the smoke and flames. The husband managed to open one of the bedroom windows and call out to neighbours in the street below. As they gathered underneath the window, he lowered his wife and children into their waiting arms. However, before he was able to make his own escape he was overcome by the smoke and choked to death. His charred body was found beside the open window when the fire had been finally brought under control.

A rebuilding programme was undertaken and new houses soon occupied the old plots. The owners of the new house built on the plot where the husband had lost his life soon began to report strange sounds coming from the upstairs room. Footsteps could be heard crossing the room and muffled shouts and coughing were also often heard. Whenever anybody went into the rooms upstairs to investigate, the footsteps always stopped but there often remained a faint smell of smoke in the air.

Today the building is used by the Strangers Club and the upstairs room has been turned into a snooker hall. Staff who have been left cleaning up downstairs after the club has closed and all the customers have gone home often report the sound of footsteps wandering around the snooker table upstairs. Whenever they venture upstairs to see if somebody has been locked in, they find only an empty room. It seems that the fire prevented the husband from leaving the room in 1507 and he's been trapped there ever since.

Just across the street from the Strangers Club is Wrights Court. At the top of the courtyard stands an antiques shop which is often visited by another ghostly presence. In the late 1800s, an outbreak of diphtheria swept through the city and left a trail of dead bodies in its wake. Unfortunately, the outbreak coincided with a strike by the local gravediggers, which meant that the bodies were not being buried. In an attempt to confine the epidemic, dead bodies were collected in groups and piled on top of each other at the back of alleyways and courtyards.

The Strangers Club, where a family were trapped during the great fire of 1507.

Such a pile built up at the end of Wrights Court. Eight bodies were stacked on top of each other; the one on the top was that of an old lady. When the gravediggers returned to work, they began collecting the bodies. When they came to Wrights Court, only seven of the eight bodies remained. The body of the old lady had simply disappeared, apparently into thin air.

If you talk to the owners of the antiques shop now situated at the top of Wrights Court, they will tell you about the shadow of an old woman that often passes by their window when they are working in the back of the shop. They hear the shop door open, the bell rings and the door closes again. The sound of footsteps can then be heard walking across the shop's wooden floor. However, when they come to serve their customer they always find the shop empty. Could it just be the old lady returning?

Towards the top of Elm Hill, the door to an old monastery remains. Set up by Father Ignatius in 1864, the monastery soon became a talking point in the city. Ignatius was not your general run-of-the-mill Sunday morning preacher. He wouldn't stand outside the door to his monastery with a plate of cakes or a pot of tea inviting you in to join him in prayer, he would stand instead with his big black Bible accosting people as they walked by. Ignatius would threaten passers-by

Wrights Court, from where an old woman's body disappeared.

The original door to the monastery of Father Ignatius.

with eternal damnation if they failed to join him inside his monastery. He told them that they would live a life of purgatory and then burn in Hell for eternity and their souls would hang from the chandeliers of the Devil's front room. All this for missing early morning prayers at Ignatius's monastery.

It was not wise to get on the wrong side of Father Ignatius. One day, a young woman passing by the monastery became involved in an argument with Ignatius. As the argument reached its climax, the young woman swore and cursed him and he cursed her back. She walked away and then fell down dead a few steps further along the Hill. Some time later, Ignatius was involved in another argument, this time with two gardeners. Again, as the argument finished, Ignatius cursed them both. The two men went off scoffing at his curses but they were both found dead in their beds the following morning.

The people of Norwich began to believe that Father Ignatius was in league with some greater power, possibly even the Devil himself and so decided to chase him from the city. They came to Elm Hill one night in July with lit torches to burn down his monastery. It was a warm summer's evening with barely a cloud in the sky and yet, as they came round the top of Elm Hill, the most torrential downpour broke out and extinguished their torches. They fled in fear, even more convinced that Ignatius had powerful 'friends'.

A few weeks later, under the cover of darkness, they returned. Breaking down the door to his monastery, they found Ignatius asleep in his bed. Before he realised what was happening, they dragged him from his bed and marched him to the outskirts of the city. There they forced him to vow, under pain of death, never to return to the city again. He made the vow and he never did return, at least not when he was alive.

Following reports of his death, however, the ghost of Father Ignatius began to be seen wandering up and down Elm Hill. Still carrying his big black Bible, he continues to curse people as they pass by.

For such a short street, Elm Hill certainly has more than its fair share of ghosts.

NINE

THE LONELY GHOST
AT NO. 19
MAGDALEN STREET

Tucked away between charity shops and restaurants, the building at No. 19 Magdalen Street may not look particularly eerie but over the last forty years it has gained the reputation of being the 'most haunted building in Norwich'.

During the 1800s, a time when it was claimed that there were enough churches in the city to visit a different one every week of the year and enough pubs to visit a different one every day, No. 19 Magdalen Street was host to the Key Merchant Arms public house. Apart from the fine ales on offer, the landlord in the 1860s ran another service for his customers. For a small fee, there was an attic room where 'gentlemen' could bring their ladies to entertain them. It was not perhaps a brothel in the strictest sense of the word but a steady stream of young ladies would accompany their gentlemen friends up and down the stairs over the course of an evening. It was from these activities that our ghost, Sarah, seems to originate.

Some 100 years later, the churches still stood but many of the public houses had become home to other businesses. The Key Merchant Arms was no exception and had become a shop around the time of the Second World War. By 1965, it was leased by Radio Rentals, who specialised in hiring out television sets and radios. It was at this time that the staff began to notice some unusual activity.

Cups of tea and coffee would begin to fall from tables and desks on a regular basis. At first, this was put down to staff clumsiness but it became so prevalent that eventually taking hot drinks out of the staffroom was banned. Despite this, the activities continued and indeed increased. Sheets of paper would mysteriously float from one desk to another, rulers and staplers would jump up and down on the desktops, but most scary of all was when an old-fashioned typewriter, one that had to be hit relatively hard to make it work, began to work when there was nobody anywhere near it. It left absolute gibberish on the paper it typed on but it was enough to make the staff plead with the management to find alternative accommodation.

Eventually, the owners relocated further along the road and No. 19 Magdalen Street awaited its new tenants. It wasn't long before Sterling Travel moved in and the mysterious goings-on soon started up once more. Again, the staff pleaded with the owners to move but this time the management were less keen to do so. The rent on the property was very reasonable and the owners of Sterling Travel were happy to stay where they were.

A few months into their occupancy, however, a strange occurrence caused them to change their minds. Late one afternoon, the owner was sitting upstairs behind his desk when he became aware that some of the clipboards hanging on the wall were beginning to sway from side to

No.19 Magdalen Street is the most haunted building in Norwich.

side. These clipboards held the details of where his drivers were to go the following day and he watched them as they continued to sway. After a short period, one of the clipboards suddenly flew from the wall to land in front of his desk. Within seconds, the others had followed and the amazed owner sat looking at the pile of clipboards lying in the centre of the room. It was then that he decided to agree to the staff's relocation requests.

After a short period when the building lay empty, the next tenants were Oxfam and this is where our story moves up a gear. The usual disturbances followed but things came to a head one evening just before closing time. An elderly gentleman arrived with five or six bin liners full of clothes. The staff didn't have time to sort them out so they took the bags upstairs and left them in the front office, the same office where the clipboards had jumped from the wall a few months earlier.

When they arrived the next morning, they found that all the bags had been turned upside down and all the clothes lay strewn across the floor – well, nearly all. Those that would have fitted a young woman had been neatly folded and piled in one corner. The staff at Oxfam were now convinced that something unusual was happening in this room and did something that may be regarded as either very brave or very stupid – they held an Ouija board session upstairs in the very same room.

At this session, a young girl by the name of Sarah revealed herself and began to send messages via the glass and alphabet laid out on the table. This is the story she told them.

The window from where Sarah was often seen looking out has been boarded up.

She had been brought to the building 100 years earlier, when it was an inn. However, she was unaware of its reputation and when her gentleman friend had invited her upstairs, she had gone with him without realising his intentions. Once alone in the upstairs room, it soon became clear what her companion was seeking and Sarah fought for her honour. Unfortunately, during the struggle that followed, Sarah was strangled by her gentleman friend and her body was left in the room. Sadly, it seems that Sarah didn't realise she was dead and couldn't understand why nobody was talking to her or taking any notice of her. This was why she had been knocking things over and moving things in an attempt to gain attention.

The Oxfam staff were so amazed at their experience that they did some research and found that a young girl had indeed been murdered in the room upstairs when the building was an inn. Her attacker had never been brought to justice. Convinced that Sarah was still in the building, the manager went to see the Bishop of Norwich and told him what had happened. After a long discussion, the Bishop agreed to exorcise the building and a few weeks later the deliverance team made its way to No. 19 Magdalen Street to carry out a bell, book and candle exorcism.

However, it seems that Sarah wasn't impressed by the exorcism and decided to stay anyway. This isn't too surprising. After all, exorcisms are usually intended to get rid of evil spirits and Sarah isn't evil, merely lost.

A few months later, Oxfam moved to larger premises and the shop became vacant again. The new tenant was Ron's Reptiles. Spiders, snakes and ghosts – a wonderful combination.

Ron was a bit of a handyman and shortly after moving in he decided to indulge in a bit of do-it-yourself. Ron installed a partition wall at the back of the shop to give him a small area for storage. It was only built from plywood with a simple door in the middle but as soon as he had completed the task he noticed something very unusual. The storeroom area he had sectioned off became incredibly cold, remaining approximately 6-7 degrees colder than the rest of the shop throughout the year. It suited Ron perfectly, as anything that had to go into hibernation could be sent straight into the back room. His dog was far more reluctant, however, refusing to cross the threshold even when being enticed with food and titbits. Ron's wife, Elizabeth, also had problems with the room, only going in whenever it was really necessary and coming out again as soon as possible. She often sensed the smell of lavender inside the room and also the impression that there was someone upstairs. It should be noted that the sectioned-off area is directly underneath the room where Sarah was murdered over 100 years ago.

Ron's Reptiles moved out after a year or so and a number of short-term tenants have followed. Strangely, none have decided to stay for more than a few months at a time. The building is currently being converted into a shop downstairs with living accommodation upstairs. Maybe the new owner doesn't believe in ghosts or maybe he's simply unaware of the building's history. Either way, it will be interesting to see how long it is before Sarah confronts him.

Sarah has been seen in the window on the wall to the room where she was murdered. It was bricked up from the inside many years ago but the window sill and frame remain on the outside of the building. Many years ago, a delivery driver bringing stock to the rear of the shop happened to glance up at the window and saw a young woman looking out of it. He mentioned this to the staff, who told him he must have been mistaken as the window had been bricked over many years earlier.

However, a few weeks later another visitor remarked on the young girl watching from the window and some time after that a member of staff also caught a glimpse of somebody behind the window frame. When reports began to circulate, the window became a local tourist attraction until it was finally boarded up from the outside.

Sarah hasn't been seen since but who's to say she won't make another appearance in the future.

The deliverance team

Every diocese in the Church of England has a deliverance team to deal with unexplained paranormal events. Often called upon to attend buildings where there are believed to be ghosts or ghostly goings-on, they work on a far more regular basis than they care to admit.

It is not the policy of the Church to either name the members of their team or to confirm the places where they have been called to visit. However, one team member who was prepared to comment admitted, 'It's not something we really care to talk about. We rather tend to play it down but we do quite a lot of work in the diocese and are called upon fairly frequently.' When pressed further, he confirmed, 'In a minority of cases there may be some experience of a person's presence. That would be a presence of a non-physical kind. The difficulty comes with what to call such an experience. If you call it a ghost, then people tend to think of someone with a white sheet over their head.'

'Performing the ministry of exorcism involves bringing peace and light where there is disturbance and darkness,' he added, finally commenting that an exorcism would only be carried out in an extremely rare case.

TEN

THE MARTYRS OF LOLLARDS PIT

If ever an area of Norwich was destined to be haunted, it would surely be Lollards Pit. Now filled in and covered over to form part of the car parks behind the Bridge Inn public house and the local car exhaust centre, the pit holds the secret to one of the darkest periods during the history of Norwich. It also holds possibly one of the largest collections of ghosts anywhere in the city.

Originally a chalk pit, it was excavated when the city's cathedral was built. All the stone used in the building of the cathedral came from France but the chalk was local. The pit was then left empty and dormant for around 300 years, until a new use was found for it. And what a dreadful use that was.

Try and picture the scene. A young girl tied to the stake as the flames lap around her ankles. She screams and struggles but the chains hold her arms tight behind her. She looks down and sees the hem of her dress as it catches fire and she feels the heat of the flames as they begin to travel up her body. She screams again, this time more desperately, but the only response she gets is the cheering and mocking of the baying crowd who watch her every agonised move with eyes that dance with excitement and mouths that are curled into evil smiles.

She begins to choke as the smoke engulfs her and she prays that it will overcome her completely before the flames take hold of her body. As she coughs and gasps for breath, she feels the flames dancing around her head and she realises her hair has now caught fire. In panic, she screams for mercy but mercy is not forthcoming. The flesh on her arms and legs begins to drip as the heat becomes more intense. Almost blinded by the smoke, she searches for a friendly face among the crowd but there are none, only taunting and cheering faces meet her gaze.

Again she prays for an early release but the only answer she gets is the pain of the flames now attacking her face, her lips, her eyes, her ears. As her dress finally explodes under the intense heat, a bellowing smoke envelopes her and she begins to choke more violently. In a few minutes she is dead, but for the mob the performance is only halfway through.

Like zombies drawn to a blood feast, they remain in the pit as the lifeless body of the young girl is ravished by the flames. As her clothes are burnt away to reveal the innocent, charred body of a young woman, they cry out with glee and offer their praises to God Almighty. As her flesh melts and her bones become visible, they bet on which arm or leg will be the first to fall to the ground. Finally, when there is nothing left except a few charred bones and a skull hanging across the chains that once held a young girl to the stake, they begin to disperse, comparing the performance against those they have witnessed on previous visits to the pit.

Some hours later, a couple of pitmen will arrive and begin the grim task of gathering up the charred bones, still warm from the heat of the flames that burnt them. Together with anything else remaining of the young girl, the bones will be buried under the ashes. A few days later, it will all happen again – another crowd, another victim, another execution in the name of God. It may seem like a Stephen King horror movie but the events took place in an old chalk pit within sight of the city cathedral and happened less than 400 years ago.

So how did it ever come to this? A local crowd cheering and laughing as men and women, young and old, were chained to a wooden stake and burnt. Fear and ignorance? Far from it – these barbaric rituals were actually a result of fear and education. Education of the common people, which had led them to start questioning the wisdom of Rome and the papacy, and the Catholic Church's fear that they had been found out.

In earlier times, it had all been so simple. You went to church each week and did as your local priest told you. His beliefs were your beliefs and you would receive your salvation at his hands and through his teaching. Now, however, in the early fifteenth century, things were not quite so clear. The local priest was being questioned and the all-powerful teachings from Rome were

A car park now covers Lollards Pit, the most infamous area of Norwich.

being called into doubt. The first translations of the Bible into English were becoming available and people who had been teaching themselves to read over the past few years were suddenly discovering that not everything they had been taught to accept by the Church was exactly what it said in the Holy Book.

The Church was worried. Seeing its power and, subsequently, its wealth under threat, it looked around anxiously for a way to retaliate. The obvious way of subduing a challenging congregation was the same as it always had been – by fear.

Their first port of call was to the King and in 1400 the bishops took their fears to Henry IV and advised him that the Church was under threat. The King was no fool and he knew that a strong Church was vital for a successful monarch and he agreed to help the bishops repress the apparent revolt. In 1401, the statute 'De Heretico Comburendo' ('The Necessity of Burning Heretics') was passed, forbidding anyone to preach or practise anything contrary to the sacrament or the authority of the Church. The punishment for anyone found guilty of breaking the new statute would be to be 'burnt before the people'.

So there it was, in black and white, a licence to burn anyone who didn't agree with what the Church preached – education to be punished with a terrible death.

The Lollards

William White

The word 'Lollard' derives from an old Dutch word meaning 'mumbler'. The Lollards were known as mumblers because, it is claimed, they used to mumble to themselves as they read through the Bible, disagreeing with the things they had been taught.

The first burning in Lollards Pit took place in 1428, when William White gained the dubious honour of being its first victim. White was a priest who had moved from Kent to Ludham in Norfolk. Upon his arrival, he began to preach to the local people on the streets of Norwich. Fervently opposed to the Roman Catholic Church, he claimed that priests and bishops had no power to grant absolution via confessions and that men should seek forgiveness for their sins at the hands of God alone. Among other things, he claimed that the Pope's Holiness was a 'Devilish estate', that men should not worship images or other idolatrous paintings or works of art and, perhaps most daringly of all, that men who wore cowls (monks' hoods) were the 'soldiers of Lucifer'.

This was hardly the stuff to endear him to the Church and White found himself hauled in front of the Archbishop of Canterbury, where he recanted. To recant was to withdraw the remarks you had made and promise to live according to the Church's rules and beliefs in future. Following the recantation, a penance had to be paid. This would often be in the form of a whipping or being made to beg forgiveness at the altar. White received the lesser punishment and spent several days kneeling at the altar, begging for forgiveness.

Back in Ludham, White regretted having recanted and began preaching on the streets once more. Again he was arrested and this time he was taken before the Bishop of Norwich to explain his actions. Again he was offered the chance to recant but this time he refused, claiming that his beliefs were too strong for him to deny them. After trying in vain to make White change his mind, the Bishop finally condemned him to death. He would be burnt alive in Lollards Pit.

In September 1428, White became the first martyr to make his way down Bishopgate and over Bishopbridge to the pit. Now seventy years old, he was led by a group of local priests and followed by a crowd both curious and excited at the approaching spectacle. White was forced to carry the very firewood that would be used to start the fire which would consume him. White carried his 'faggot' of firewood across his shoulders as he made his way slowly down the street to his death.

Becoming more excited, the crowd began to hurl rotting fruit and vegetables and even eggs at White, in the same manner as they would at those who were placed in the pillory or stocks in the city. But perhaps the greatest indignity came at the end of Bishopgate, as those living in the houses towards the bridge went upstairs, opened their bedroom windows and emptied the contents of their chamberpots over him as he passed by.

Whether or not this was a sign of their hatred or merely their way of showing the authorities that they did not support the same views as those who were burnt in the pit is unknown. Whatever the reason, local martyrs were regularly treated in this manner and it was to be seen many times over the next 150 years.

Bishopbridge, over which Lollards and witches were dragged to their deaths.

The Guildhall, where Thomas Bilney demonstrated his faith.

Thomas Bilney

Possibly the most famous martyr to be burnt at Lollards Pit was Thomas Bilney. The story of Bilney is referred to in Foxe's *Book of Martyrs*, accompanied with an illustration taken from the Guildhall in Norwich.

Little is known of Bilney's early life other than that he was born in 1495 and spent most of his early life in the village of Bilney. There is, therefore, the distinct possibility that he may have changed his surname to that of his birthplace at some time or another. This would account for the singular lack of records of his early years in the small village.

What is known for definite is that Bilney entered Trinity Hall, Cambridge when very young, possibly as young as eighteen or nineteen. Just a few years later, at the age of twenty-four, he was ordained a priest by Nicholas West, Bishop of Ely.

It appears that, shortly after being ordained, Bilney discovered a Greek version of the New Testament which, he believed, revealed the truth of free salvation by the faith of Jesus. Finding the teachings quite different to those of the Catholic Church, Bilney devoured the book and spent almost every waking hour reading and re-reading it until he became convinced of its truth. Perhaps more importantly, he also became convinced that he had been chosen to spread this new faith.

Slowly, he began to convert many of his friends and colleagues to his way of thought and, encouraged by his success, he set out to preach this new gospel to the public at large. It was a journey that would lead him to a tragic end.

Bilney left Cambridge and began to spread his beliefs among the poor, the sick and even the lepers. His friends looked on in horror as he stayed for days at a time in the leper houses, preaching his new-found faith and attempting to convert these already condemned men.

In 1527, after giving a sermon at Christ Church, Ipswich, he was arrested and imprisoned. A few days later, he was taken before the Bishop of London. He was urged to disown his beliefs and recant. Despite repeated pressure over the next ten days, he refused but when his friends visited him they convinced him he could serve more good alive than by becoming a martyr at the stake.

As a penance, he was held in prison until the following year. He was then released and told to return to Cambridge. A condition of his release was that he was forbidden from preaching but Bilney had regretted his recantation almost as soon as he had carried it out and now, free once again, he could no longer subdue the urge to carry on spreading the gospel of Christ as he understood it.

In 1529, he made his way to Norwich. He began to wait outside churches, preaching to the congregations as they came out. He was quickly brought before Bishop Nixe at the Bishop's Palace. Nixe was a staunch Catholic and urged Bilney to recant his beliefs once more. This time, Bilney refused and the Bishop had him imprisoned while he sent for a writ to burn him. When the writ arrived, Bishop Nixe again urged Bilney to recant but still he refused. Bilney was tried for heresy, found guilty and condemned to be burnt alive in the pit.

The night before his burning, he was held in the Guildhall in Norwich's marketplace, where his friends visited him for the last time. Despite their feelings of despair, he tried to convince them that he was happy and willing to die for his beliefs. To demonstrate his faith, he lit a candle and held his hand over the flame. As his friends looked on in disbelief, he allowed the flame to consume one of his fingers before he withdrew his hand. It is this illustration that appears in Foxe's *Book of Martyrs*.

The following day, Bilney was taken to the pit and addressed the crowd: 'Good people! I am come hither to die.' He then went on to list his beliefs, before removing his gown and making his way to the stake. There he knelt on the small ledge where he was to stand and prayed. Having composed himself, he asked the officers if they were ready and, after they had confirmed to him that they were, he removed his jacket and doublet and stood upon the ledge in front of the stake while the officers wrapped the chains around him.

The fire was then lit beneath him and he began to pray as he awaited his fate. However, the wind was so strong that day that it blew the flames away from his body. What this meant was that Bilney was getting very, very hot but he wasn't actually burning. One report at the time described his flesh as 'bubbling'; he was being slowly cooked alive. Finally, one of the officers on duty took pity on him and knocked out the staple holding the stake in the ground, allowing it to fall forward. As Bilney fell into the flames, he was heard to cry out 'Jesus, I believe!'

A few moments later, the same officer placed a burning faggot on his lifeless back to help the flames consume the rest of his body.

Lollards Pit under the reign of Queen Mary

In 1553, following the death of Edward VI, Mary came to the throne of England. It is no accident that by the end of her five-year reign she had acquired the nickname of 'Bloody Mary'.

Queen Mary was a staunch Catholic and believed that all the progress made by the Church of England and the Protestant believers should be undone as quickly as possible.

She swiftly renounced the title of Supreme Head of the Church of England and committed the country back to the faith of Rome. Those who didn't share her beliefs were mercilessly dealt with as the greatest tide of burning of heretics in the history of England began. As if this unforgiving reign of terror wasn't enough, Norwich was to have an extra burden to bear. When the appointment of Dr John Hopton as Bishop of Norwich was announced, the local Protestants must have shuddered with fear.

Hopton had been confessor to the Queen when she was Princess Mary and was one of the most devout Catholics throughout the kingdom. His appointment as Bishop of Norwich must have come as a dreadful blow to the many Protestants who lived in the area. When Hopton appointed Dr Dunning as his chancellor, an alliance as dreadful as anything that could be imagined was put into place. Dunning's hatred of nonconforming Catholics was even greater than that of Hopton.

Over the next few years, Hopton and Dunning earned their reputations as the most feared religious judges in the country. They condemned and executed without mercy, although this was often not enough to satisfy the crazed bloodlust the two men developed.

A simple burning was not enough for most of the victims. Most were severely tortured and degraded over the period leading up to their deaths. Many of their victims must have made their

The plaque on the riverside commemorating the Lollards burnt in the pit on the other side of the road.

way to Lollards Pit thankful that their agonies were about to end. Heretics convicted by either Hopton or Dunning spent the days between conviction and burning tied to a stake either at the Bishop's Palace, the Guildhall or the castle. Their hands were drawn high above their heads and bound to chains in the ceiling, leaving them to spend the entire period standing on tiptoe.

Their daily feed was three spoonfuls of water and a small piece of bread, fed to them by the local gaoler. They spent the entire period, twenty-four hours a day, on tiptoe and tied to the stake. The bread was pushed into their mouths, leaving them to try and swallow as much as possible. The bits they dropped were eaten by the rats that shared their cells; this at least gave them a temporary reprieve from the constant gnawing of their feet by the rats that they suffered as they hung from the ceiling. It is hard to imagine the pain that these poor souls must have suffered in the days leading up to the day of their burning.

Possibly the cruellest burning that ever took place in the pit was that of a young woman in 1557. Despite being heavily pregnant, the woman, who had been convicted of heresy, was tied to the stake and set alight. As the flames swept over her body, the woman went into labour and actually gave birth while tied to the stake. The child was allowed to fall into the flames, where it burnt to death along with its mother. There is no record of whether the child was male or female.

There are no definite figures detailing how many Lollards suffered at the hands of Hopton and Dunning. A plaque on the riverside opposite the pit lists the names of eight martyrs who suffered during the reign of Queen Mary. Foxe's *Book Of Martyrs* lists maybe a dozen more, but perhaps the most damning evidence comes from the cathedral's own records, which can be found in the small cathedral library. These records list the number of burnings taking place as six in 1555, twelve in 1556, twenty-nine in 1557 and seventeen in 1558, the year Mary died. It also offers the information that this was the highest number of burnings recorded during this period in any town in the country except London or Canterbury.

The ghosts of Lollards Pit

Surely no other place in the city of Norwich can hold such dreadful secrets of unrelenting terror as Lollards Pit. It's little wonder that people still claim to hear the screams of pain and terror as they pass the old pit. The sound of whimpering made by the ghosts of those poor souls is also often heard. Some people even claim to experience a sudden rush of heat as they make their way from one side of the car park to the other, a heat reminiscent of the flames that used to burn in the pit beneath.

There are no reported sightings of any of the poor souls who perished there. There is, however, that constant moaning and groaning that can be heard coming from below the ground at night. How many trapped souls remain below the ashes may never be known, but Lollards Pit will forever remain a stain on the history of the city.

The witches

There are many people who will tell you that we never burnt witches in this country. They will tell you that all our convicted witches were hanged and any who may have been burnt were actually burnt for heresy and not witchcraft. Ask them, then, to explain the documentation in

Fye Bridge. This was where the 'cucking' stool was used to condemn witches.

the cathedral which confirms the burning of Mary Oliver in the Castle Ditches in 1659 for practising 'the art of witchcraft'.

It is true we didn't burn as many witches as our European friends. The French, the Italians and even the Belgians burnt a lot more witches than us; we did indeed hang most of our witches. But we burnt our fair share as well.

Once a woman had been accused of witchcraft, her chances of survival were slim. Her body was examined for telltale marks of the Devil and, if these were not found, many other tests would be used to 'prove' she was indeed dabbling in the craft of Wicca.

Sometimes, it was enough to claim you had seen the woman talking to a familiar – any kind of small, black animal or bird – and then a few moments later experienced a pain of some description. It would then be deduced that the woman had used her familiar to cast a spell upon you.

One of the more common forms of trial was to duck the poor woman in the river in a 'cucking stool' on Fye Bridge. The woman would be left under the river for an undetermined length of time, after which she would be hauled back out again to see if she had survived. If she was dead, then she was deemed to be innocent – a little late, some may feel. If, on the other hand, she was still alive then she was deemed to be guilty and she'd either be hanged or burnt alive in the pit.

Furthermore, it is believed that if a particularly attractive young girl was accused of witchcraft when there were visiting dignitaries to the city, then the young girl would be ducked in the river for a very short period of time, ensuring that when she surfaced she would still be alive. It is hard to believe but 350 years ago it was looked upon as something of an honour to burn a pretty young woman to death for the pleasure of your visiting dignitaries.

Having been found guilty of witchcraft, the poor woman would be taken back to the Bishop's Palace, where she would be condemned to die. Sometimes she would be kept overnight in the dungeons below Cow Tower and she would begin her walk to death the following morning. Her final trail would be along Bishopgate and over Bishopbridge to the pit, following in the footsteps of the local Lollards. Some years later, these burnings were moved to the Castle Ditches, where poor Mary Oliver became the last victim.

Sometimes, these poor women would be denied any kind of trial at all. When the self-proclaimed Witchfinder General, Matthew Hopkins, visited Norwich in July 1645, he oversaw the trial of forty witches at the Norwich Assizes. Some might have found the proceedings unnecessary, as twenty of those accused had already been executed.

Not many records of the burning of witches survive; they simply weren't thought important enough for records to be kept. However, one record that does exist in the cathedral library tells of a particularly unpleasant episode.

Towards the end of the 1500s, four young women were burnt as witches at the same time in Lollards Pit. When the faggots of firewood were lit, the flames burnt through the ropes holding one of the young women to the stake before she was dead. Gasping for breath, she managed to climb, crawl and scramble out of the pit. You might think that in the late 1500s, in a country as religious and superstitious as England, the authorities would have seen this as an act of God and allowed the young woman to live. You would have to think again. As the young woman reached

The ghost of a witch still wanders up and down Bishopgate with her faggot of firewood.

the edges of the pit, the crowd picked her up and threw her back in. It is recorded that she crawled out a total of four times and each time the crowd threw her back into the pit, where she finally burnt to death.

A bailiff on duty on that particular day was horrified by the events and stated that it should never happen again. From that day on, witches were chained to the stake.

There is a legend that the ghost of one of the condemned witches still wanders up and down Bishopgate carrying the faggot of firewood used to set her alight. Dressed in rags and seemingly oblivious to her surroundings, she mumbles as she makes her way from one end of the street to the other. On occasions, she has been known to drop her firewood and plead for help in picking it up again. It is said that should you ever see her and help her with her bundle of sticks, then you will die in a fire within six months.

ELEVEN

THE DUMPLING POISONER

The large Roman Catholic cathedral church standing at the top of what used to be known as Gallows Hill was commissioned by the Duke of Norfolk in 1877. On occasions, a middle-aged gentleman has been seen wandering around the church and the surrounding area carrying what appears to be a bag of flour. However, this gentleman does not seem to be somebody coming to the church to make a donation. Indeed, he appears to belong to a different century altogether.

Prior to the building of the church, the site spent most of the 1800s occupied by the city gaol. In the mid 1820s, when the gaol was almost complete, it was decided that a new gallows would be ordered and the authorities looked for a carpenter/blacksmith to build it. The man chosen was John Stratford, who was delighted to get the job. He joked to friends that he would now secure his place in history as the man who had built the gallows for the new gaol. Little did he know that his place in history was to be secured by a much more ironic method.

On the face of it, John Stratford was as unlikely a murderer as you might ever meet. Apprenticed as a young man to a local blacksmith, he later took over the ownership of the Swan public house in King Street, Norwich. When this didn't pay, he reverted to his trade as a 'smiffy' and moved into a small house in St Faiths Lane, from where he traded. Life was, if anything, a little mundane in the Stratford household and Stratford lived in relative anonymity with his wife and their six children. However, when the job of building the gallows came along, Stratford believed life was looking up.

In 1828, through a mutual friend, Stratford met Jane Briggs, a woman often described as 'beholding to the eye'. Briggs' husband, Thomas, was living as a pauper in the Norwich workhouse and had been in ill health for some time. A friendship between Stratford and Jane blossomed and in the early weeks of 1829 Jane informed Stratford that she was carrying his child. Stratford was horrified by the news and terrified at the prospect of his wife and family becoming aware of the secret liaison. He urged Jane to end the pregnancy and even provided her with some powder which he claimed would abort the unborn child. Jane, however, had very different ideas and threw the powder away, informing Stratford that she had no intention of getting rid of the baby.

Stratford knew that Jane had not slept with her husband since he had been admitted to the workhouse and obviously he would know the child was not his. Stratford became convinced that Thomas Briggs would discover that he was the father of his wife's child and that he would expose him. He therefore had to get rid of Thomas Briggs.

A plot was hatched and Stratford took some flour laced with arsenic to the workhouse and left it as an anonymous gift for Briggs. Briggs, however, already had quite a supply of flour and therefore left the 'gift' unopened for some time. Another inmate, John Burgess, who was living in the workhouse with his family, discovered the flour and took it for his own use, cooking a large dumpling for himself and his family.

Shortly after, Burgess and his entire family were taken violently ill and a doctor was called. The doctor soon diagnosed the illness as arsenic poisoning and began to administer treatment to the family. The rest of Burgess's family soon began to recover but Burgess, who had eaten the largest portion of the dumpling, failed to respond to the treatment and died in agony a few days later.

An investigation began and the wife of John Burgess soon admitted that her husband had taken the flour from another inmate's locker. When she identified the owner of the other locker as Thomas Briggs, the police turned their attention to him. Briggs explained that the flour had been left as an anonymous gift and the authorities began to question the nurse who had taken it from the anonymous donor. It wasn't long before John Stratford was identified as the person who had brought in the flour and he was arrested and put on trial for murder.

Throughout his trial, Stratford maintained his innocence and refused to answer any questions that were put to him. When asked to make his defence, he simply stated, 'Oh, I am perfectly innocent of the charges.' Despite the urgings of the judge, Stratford refused to be drawn any further. Not surprisingly, the jury quickly found him guilty and, donning the black cap, the judge passed the death sentence upon him. Stratford was then taken back to the city gaol where he would be kept until a hangman was found to carry out the sentence.

The day before his execution, Stratford was visited by his wife and six children. One of the children, a daughter aged four, threw her arms around his neck and begged him to come home for tea. There are no recorded visits from Jane Burgess. After his family had left him, Stratford asked for the governor to visit him. When he arrived, the governor told Stratford that a hangman

The Roman Catholic cathedral church, where a stranger often arrives with a parcel of flour.

had been found and that the execution would take place the following morning as planned. Stratford then told the governor that he wished to give a full confession and make his peace with God.

The governor went to fetch pen and paper and then returned with the chaplain and proceeded to take Stratford's confession. While the confession confirmed the prosecution's case and proved Stratford's guilt beyond doubt, it did lack one or two pertinent points. Stratford showed no remorse for his actions whatsoever and John Burgess, the innocent victim of Stratford's crime, wasn't even mentioned. Having unburdened himself of his guilt, if not his regret, Stratford bade the governor and chaplain goodnight and went to bed for his final night's sleep. He appeared to sleep well and seemed resigned to his forthcoming fate the following day.

The following morning, Monday 17 August 1829, crowds began to gather outside the city gaol before 7.00 a.m. The gallows had been erected on the gaol roof and the gathering crowd began to train their eyes upon it. By the time the executioner entered Stratford's cell at around 7.45 a.m., the crowd had grown to several thousand strong. The narrow space in front of the gaol was packed and the crowds stretched back along St Giles Street as far as it was possible to be and still catch a glimpse of the gallows. Every window and roof of the neighbouring houses appeared packed with faces and even the battlements of the St Giles' church steeple were crowded with spectators.

A few minutes before 8.00 a.m., Stratford arrived at the foot of the ladder leading to the scaffold, where he knelt and spent some moments in prayer. As he rose to his feet, the minister began to recite a prayer he had written especially for the occasion. At this point, Stratford began to climb the ladder and, when he reached the scaffold, he looked down upon the thousands of spectators who had come to witness his last moments on earth. Politely and deferentially, he bowed slowly three times to them.

The hangman stepped forward and began to adjust the rope around Stratford's neck. As he did so, Stratford complained that he was putting it on the wrong way but was assured by the hangman that this was not the case. The hood was drawn over his face and Stratford appeared to finally resign himself to his fate. The chaplain began to recite the Lord's Prayer, during which a handkerchief was dropped as a signal to the hangman and he immediately drew the fatal bolt. Stratford's body lurched downwards and for a few seconds the arms and legs continued to twitch, then all was still. The silence of the crowd was broken by a solitary scream – perhaps from Stratford's wife or maybe Jane Briggs, who was still carrying his unborn child – and then all was silent again.

As the crowd looked on, the man who only a few months earlier had been seen as a law-abiding citizen but would forever more be known as the Norfolk Dumpling Poisoner, died as a murderer on the very gallows he was proud to have built a few years before. He was, in fact, the very first person to have been hanged on them. Thus was the irony of John Stratford's greatest claim to fame.

Many years later, after the gaol had been knocked down and replaced with the Roman Catholic cathedral church, it seems that John Stratford returned to the place of his death. The first person to encounter him was a woman working at a garden fête organised by the Duke of Norfolk. The fête was held on 17 August, the anniversary of Stratford's hanging. The woman saw a man enter the church carrying what appeared to be a bag of flour and, assuming it had been brought to be sold at the fête, asked him to place it on the table at the side of the entrance. She turned away for a moment and when she turned back both the man and the bag of flour had disappeared. Over the years, many more sightings followed and the man always disappeared, taking his flour with him. Maybe that's not such a bad thing – who knows what would happen to anybody who came into possession of the flour and decided to use it?

TWELVE

A Tower and a Cemetery

The Rosary Road Cemetery

The cemetery along Rosary Road is the oldest common cemetery in the country. 'Common' means that people from all faiths and denominations can be buried alongside each other and Rosary Road has a wide range of 'tenants'. Ex-Lord Mayors of the city lie side by side with young men killed by gas in the First World War trenches. Merchants and notaries lie head to head and even relations of novelist Anna Sewell, of Black Beauty fame, lie there.

Cemeteries would seem to be an obvious location for ghosts to gather and yet few are reported. However, one ghost does seem to wander around the graves at Rosary Road. Maybe the most famous sighting of him dates back to the early 1960s, when an American lady was visiting her relations in Norfolk.

The woman knew that her great-great-great-grandfather lay buried in the Rosary Road cemetery and she decided to visit his grave. She intended to tidy it up a bit and then take some photos to show 'the folks back home'. Arriving at the cemetery, she was surprised at how large it was and, never having been there before, began to search in vain for the gravestone she was looking for. After half an hour or so, a friendly voice addressed her from behind and she turned to see a man holding a spade standing behind her. He introduced himself and told her he was a gardener. She explained to him that she was on vacation to the city and was looking for her great-great-great-grandfather's grave and the gardener asked her for his name. When she told him, he smiled and said he knew where her great-great-great-grandfather lay and offered to show her.

On the way to the grave, the two became involved in a conversation, during which the gardener told the woman that he had been at the cemetery for a very long time and almost looked upon his work now as a hobby. He had been there so long he knew where all the graves were. He lived nearby and it was very handy for him. The woman laughed and pointed out that it seemed a very strange hobby to have. When they reached the grave, the gardener left the woman to tidy it up and take a few photos. She bade him farewell and thanked him for his help.

Some time later, having completed the job she came for, the American lady made her way out of the cemetery. As she got close to the gates, she saw what she believed to be her gardener friend and went over to say goodbye. However, when she got there she found the person was a different gardener to the one who had helped her. She explained that she had wanted to thank his colleague and he replied that there was nobody else working in the cemetery that day. She remarked that he must be mistaken, as the other gardener had introduced himself and told her that he lived nearby.

The second gardener asked her what name the mysterious stranger had given her and she replied, 'He said his name was Joe Torris.' The second gardener smiled and told her that he did indeed know who she was talking about and it was true that he lived nearby. He offered to show her and led her a little way along the path. After a few yards, he stopped and pointed to

The gravestone under which Old Joe Torris lives.

the gravestone in front of him. It read: 'Here lies Joe Torris who died in 1849'. He told her she wasn't the first person to have met Old Joe and he doubted she would be the last. No doubt she returned to America with a better story than she could ever have hoped for.

The Cow Tower

Set along the riverside, just down from Bishopbridge, is the Cow Tower. The tower used to form part of the city defences and was set on the bend of the river to enable soldiers to watch for invaders from both directions at the same time. That part of the city wall has long gone but the tower remains one of the best preserved buildings in the city from the period when it was built. During the rebellion of Robert Kett, the tower became a strategic landmark and changed hands many times.

At the end of the rebellion, it is claimed that many of Kett's men were bricked up alive behind temporary walls inside the tower. It is said that they were chained to the original walls and simply left to starve to death. It is a fact that many human bones have been found around the edges of the tower over the years.

The tower is, of course, haunted, not by one of Kett's men but by a soldier from the Middle Ages. Little is known about the tower's ghost other than the fact that his name is Blunderkist. He is believed to have died on Christmas Eve during one of the many battles that took place in the city. Ever since, it is claimed, Blunderkist has returned on his horse every Christmas Eve to ride around the tower four times warning people that there is a war on. Dressed in armour, he gallops around the tower crying out to anybody there to 'Beware, the forces are coming!'

The Cow Tower used to be known as the Dungeon Tower and there is indeed a dungeon underneath it. It's where witches and Lollards were often kept the night before their execution. After spending their last night alive in the dungeon, they were taken before the Bishop the following morning at the Bishop's Palace. There, their death sentences were confirmed and they began their last journey to the pit along the riverside.

The name Cow Tower appears to date from the mid 1800s. Legend has it that during this period a cow managed to escape from nearby grazing fields and got inside the tower, whereupon she climbed the stairs to the very top. It took six men to carry her all the way down again and, ever since, it has been known as the Cow Tower.

Cow Tower. Blunderkist rides his horse around the tower every Christmas Eve.

Other local titles published by The History Press

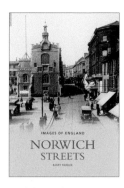

Norwich Streets

BARRY PARDUE

Enclosed by the city's medieval walls, the streets of Norwich are steeped in history. Some carry the name of ancient inns, such as the Red Lion and Ten Bells, many are a reminder of prominent citizens and others reflect the occupation of the residents. This book is illustrated with over 110 photographs and examines the way in which the street names of Norwich reflect the fortunes and misfortunes of this fascinating city.

0 7524 3505 1

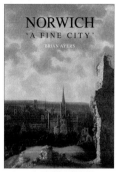

Norwich: 'A Fine City'

BRIAN AYERS

Brian Ayers shows how the city of Norwich has developed over the last 1,000 years, highlighting in particular the Norman castle and cathedral, the numerous medieval churches, the importance of Dutch 'Stranger' immigrants for post-medieval prosperity, and the buildings of the great Victorian industries.

0 7524 2549 8

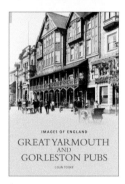

Great Yarmouth and Gorleston Pubs

COLIN TOOKE

This collection of 200 archive images recalls the intriguing history of many of Great Yarmouth and Gorleston's pubs, some of them still trading, others long since closed or demolished. Some of the pubs featured include the Feathers, with its facilities for market traders, and the Marine, with its association with oysters. This book is essential reading for all those interested in the history of Great Yarmouth and Gorleston.

0 7524 3298 2

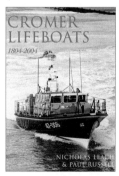

Cromer Lifeboats 1804-2004

NICHOLAS LEACH AND PAUL RUSSELL

Since 1804, a lifeboat has been stationed at Cromer ready to go to the aid of ships in distress off the Norfolk coast. The crews who have manned the Cromer lifeboat have a record of gallantry second to none and this comprehensive book encompasses the history of the station from its establishment up to the present day. Today's lifeboat crews continue the tradition of rescue at sea in the twenty-first century.

0 7524 3197 8

If you are interested in purchasing other books published by The History Press, or in case you have difficulty finding any of our books in your local bookshop, you can also place orders directly through our website
www.thehistorypress.co.uk